MORE THOUGHTS ON SCOTT WHITLOCK

"Scott Whitlock is an excellent story teller. He is and always will be an intense, passionate, master motivator, a great softball coach, exhausting, hard headed, and one of the best friends I will ever have."

Bill Gray, *Kennesaw State Assistant Softball Coach (2002-2008)*

"Behind that quick, Southern wit, lies a superior intellect and competitive nature that would have made Scott a total success in any sport or endeavor that he pursued. In addition to all of that, he was a pure pleasure to work with; totally cooperative, loyal, and humorous."

Dave Waples, *Kennesaw State University Director of Athletics (1987-2010)*

"I will be forever thankful for our 13 years together. Scott and I learned from each other and accomplished so much. I would do it again 100 times over and wouldn't change a thing. Well, maybe I would have turned that fire hydrant off a bit quicker—or maybe not."

Don McKinlay, *Kennesaw State Assistant Softball Coach (1989-2002)*

I WASN'T EXPECTING ALL THIS

MEMOIR OF A GRATEFUL COACH

SCOTT WHITLOCK
WITH JASON BROWN

Cover designed by Robert Smith

All photos courtesy of the author with the exception of the following:

Cover photo by Susan Whitlock

Interior designed by Jason Brown

First Edition

ISBN: 978-1-7332389-1-5

Printed in the United States of America

The Library of Congress Cataloging-in-Publication Data is available upon request.

DEDICATION

*I dedicate this memoir to every person who sacrificed of himself or herself in order for me to enjoy what has been an incredible journey —especially, **my family**. Beginning as far back as the date of my birth in 1961, people have done without so that I could have a better life and career.*

I have never accomplished one thing on my own, and I am both aware and appreciative of what others did (and did not do) to help me along the way. I am a lucky man.

I want to thank you all. May God Almighty bless each of you as richly as he blessed me by placing each of you in my life.

Please enjoy reading these scribbles.

CONTENTS

Foreword   ix

Introduction   xiii

PART I
PEOPLE I'VE KNOWN

1. Memories of Home   3
2. Pa-Pa   11
3. Don McKinlay and Me   17
4. The King and I   25
5. Jav   33
6. Brother from Another Mother   41
7. Bill Hill   59
8. March 21, 2013; a Sad Day   63
9. Dr. Bobbie Bailey   69
10. Lexi   75
11. Three Old Men   83

PART II
THINGS I'VE LEARNED

12. Coaching is Not for Sissies   99
13. We Have a Mess on Our Hands   107
14. "Mister, You Are 100 Percent Right."   129
15. Dyan Sets Me Straight   137
16. Be Careful of What You Ask—They Just Might   141
    Answer You
17. You Can Learn a Lot Sitting on Wooden Benches   145
18. Dawg for a Day   151
19. "What a Little Ole Five-Game Winning Streak   163
    Can Do."
20. The Day Billy Graham Died   203

PART III
LAUGHS I'VE SHARED

21. Jack MacKay's Advice on Public Speaking   207

22. Working for The King   213

23. "Coach, You're Going to Have a Problem."   219

24. Bad Oysters Are No Joke   223

25. "Scott, I Think That I Could've Took Her."   231

Afterword   237

Acknowledgments   247

About the Author   277

About the Editor   279

FOREWORD

BY MIKE CANDREA

Life works in mysterious ways and you never know when you will have the opportunity to meet someone special. Now, I need to expand upon the use of "special" in this case. Special as in unique, different, humorous, talented, caring, and humble. These could be some of the adjectives that would help me describe a great friend, associate, and definitely someone who has become a member of our family. Joel Scott Whitlock, whom you are about to get to know though the following pages of this book, is one of the most loyal and gracious people I have ever had the pleasure to meet.

I will never forget the first time I had the chance to meet Coach Whitlock. He was a very successful softball coach at Kennesaw State University. I was not very familiar with Kennesaw State, but became well aware of their successful softball program lead by one of the most successful college coaches in the game. I had followed their success over numerous years and admired the consistency of excellence they had over many years. I knew that anyone who could have this continued success, had to be a damn good coach, great with student-athletes, and a great teacher of the game.

The good Lord gave me the opportunity to meet Coach Whitlock at our coaches convention where he was receiving one of his many Coach of the Year Awards. I must say that I was impressed with his delivery of his acceptance speech as he was thankful, humorous, and very grounded! I was so impressed, I asked Scott to speak at one of my coaches clinics. After numerous phone calls, I knew he was as genuine as they come. He thought I wanted him to *attend* the clinic as a participant and I finally had to explain to him that I wanted him to be one of the speakers. Little would I know, that clinic would provide me with one of my best friends for life!

I am quite sure you will enjoy reading this collection of "Whitlock" stories, and man does he ever have some stories. I have never met a man that can tell a story like Scott Whitlock! I have had the pleasure of listening to his jokes and stories over the years and realized that I would laugh immediately because of his facial expressions and that great Southern accent. I could always count on Scott to lighten up even the most intense situation—and boy, we have gone through a few in our coaching careers. I am sure his ability to communicate, provide some humor, and make good decisions has made him a great administrator for all these years. I have never met a person that did not enjoy spending time with Scott other than our friend Javier Vela. I have waited for years to see Jav tear into Scott for his constant humorous remarks about his friend. My camps and clinics would not be the same without Scott, Jav, and Bull. Scott's truck driving experience from his youth days has come in handy since he is not very good with physical work! That is where Bull and Jav make up for Scott's weaknesses. After all, he is definitely not perfect!

I am honored to have the opportunity to write this foreword for the next *best seller*. You see, Scott is family and when family calls...you answer the bell. My Italian heritage has taught me the importance of three things—the Yankees, family, and red sauce! Family is always the center of our life and I have been blessed to have Scott and Susan at my side for the great times and some tough times life can bring. I always know that our friendship will be forever.

I did mention that Scott was a very humble man who loves his family. Joel Scott Whitlock has had a tremendous coaching career and he does not like to talk about his accomplishments. One day I asked Scott what area in the game that he felt was his expertise. I was expecting one of the many skill sets involved in the game, but he humbly blurted out—"WINNING!" Hard to argue that point and all I can say is I totally agree! My father told me that I would have many acquaintances in life, but if you can have a handful of true friends, you are very blessed. Well, I have been blessed to have Scott and Susan in my life and they will always have a place close to my heart.

I hope you enjoy this collection of Scott Whitlock stories as much as I have enjoyed my time with him. I promise you that he was brought into my life for a reason. I am quite sure that after you read his stories, you will make it a point to meet him in person! He's one of a kind and I'm proud to call him my friend!

PS: Scott demanded that I write at least three pages on his greatness, but this is all I could come up with—and still feel good about him!

INTRODUCTION

SELF ASSESSMENT

Why in the world would I write a book? Better yet, why in the world would anyone want to read something that I've written? Both are good questions, but I'll try to answer only the first. I will leave the second for you to ponder.

During my near six decades of living, I have seen a lot. I have enjoyed professional success. I have felt the joy of reaching the pinnacle of my profession and have suffered through the slings and arrows that come with failure and the unrealistic expectations of others.

My personal ledger has also had both high and low entries. I'll never forget the day my granddaughter was born, nor shall I forget the night that I was told my grandfather was gone. Just as in work, within my personal life I have experienced the highs of pure, unabridged happiness and I have also felt the horrible, *shot in the gut* feeling that comes only when one takes time to realize they have hurt or failed a loved one.

In writing this book, I am trying to share a portion of what I have learned, experienced, and become.

* * *

I suppose when you write a book biographical in nature, readers expect to walk away having a better idea of who the author really is. That very expectation in and of itself causes me great trepidation. I hope when you get a better idea of who I am, you won't be too disappointed.

OK, let's get this over with. This is me:

When alone, I am a very dull, predictable creature. I watch the same TV reruns over and over, I only have four or five meals that I really like, I can be moody, I love the music of Hank Williams Sr., I hate that the outcomes of pro wrestling matches are basically predetermined, and I am hooked on Coca-Cola.

I hate to be alone. I'm always uneasy, even downright nervous, when another's voice is not readily available to me. It's not that I need someone sitting by me every minute, but I function much better when I am not by myself. I am sure that there is some psychological definition for that, but the need for companionship is a major part of my insides.

When I am in the company of another—especially if I like them—a light comes on inside me. I come alive. The insecurities, to which I just confessed, vanish. Maybe that's why I have always loved being a part of a team.

Please don't get the wrong idea. I am a happy, grateful man. My life has been great. I am one of the luckiest people ever to draw a breath. I was loved and cared for as a child, I have countless friends, I have a beautiful family, and I have enjoyed a fairy-tale career.

One of my best assets is the knack of having great timing. It seems that every time I've needed something good to happen to me, I've always been in a place that would allow it. Another of my strengths is throughout my life I've managed to keep a fairly good sense of humor and not take myself too seriously. I love to laugh and to hear the laughter of others. However...

With all due respect to *good timing* and a *sense of humor*, my top attribute is that I have always found myself surrounded by *extraordinary people*. For some reason, God has always provided me, *regardless of circumstance*, with *someone*. *Someone* who prevents the insecurities, as described earlier, from rearing their ugly mugs. *Someone* who helps me succeed, *someone* who believes in me, and *SOMEONE* who will tell me when I am wrong (such a person we all need). God has seen to it that *someone* has always been there for me.

Thinking about it now, perhaps this project is just an effort to publicly say "thank you" to the Good Lord and to the *some-ones* who have provided me with (what has been for the most part) an enjoyable ride over life's bumpy road.

I hope you enjoy this collection of thoughts and recollections. You may not believe some of these stories, but they are all true.

Thanks.

Scott

PART I

PEOPLE I'VE KNOWN

MEMORIES OF HOME

I come from Bostwick, Georgia (30623), a small rural town of under 1,000 people. I mention the ZIP code because my beloved grandmother, Mozelle K. Whitlock, was the postmaster there for 37 years, and her teaching me 3-0-6-2-3 is one of my fondest childhood memories of her. She was so proud when I mastered it.

The Bostwick I grew up in was a modest place full of wonderful people. I was born in late November of 1961. For the first 18 years of my life, that little town and its citizens were all I knew. When John Ruark and I left for Tifton to start college in September of 1979, I had no idea what I was leaving. Now that I have been away for 35+ years, I have grown to realize how lucky I am to be a native of the little town that sits between Madison and Monroe on Highway 83.

* * *

The Last Time I Messed with Cheryl

The following occurred when I was about 10 years old, so that would have made my sister Cheryl about 5. John Ruark and I were playing basketball in my backyard and Cheryl was playing in the yard, too. Though I do not completely recollect what, Cheryl did something to aggravate me, and I pushed her down. I then found out just how cold and calculating Cheryl can be (remember, she was only 5).

After I pushed her down and went back to playing basketball, Cheryl went over and picked up an old broom handle that was at the edge of our yard. Then, she *waited*. Like a paid assassin in an alleyway, she waited for her moment to strike. When I had to bend over (much too near her for my own well-being) to retrieve the basketball, she pounced. Wham! She let me have it right across the back of my head with that broom handle. I have never bothered my little sister since, and to this day, if she goes near a broom, I leave the room.

* * *

On a serious note, my sister Cheryl is a woman of character and faith whom I love and admire greatly. I'll never be able to repay her for being there day-in, day-out to care for our grandmother in her declining years. Her being there, and my knowing it, allowed me to push my career along. I could not have done so without her. I owe her so much.

Cheryl is a most likable gal, full of personality. She's a good wife to her husband, David, and a great mom to Brittany and Chelsea.

* * *

John Lill Visits the Fair Play Game Room

My favorite John Lill story did not actually occur in Bostwick. It didn't even happen in Georgia. It took place in Fair Play, South Carolina. Fair Play is a bump in the road near Lake Hartwell, just across the state line. The town really wasn't (and still isn't) much of anything, but in 1978 it had a game room/pool hall. It was in that pool room that John Lill, and his hard head, nearly got both of us killed.

I was invited to John's family's lake house for the weekend. John, his little brother Ken, and I had spent the day having Mr. and Mrs. Lill pull us all over that lake on water skis. After dinner, John and I were looking for something to do. We decided to drive the four or so miles required to get us to the Fair Play Game Room. John and I loved to shoot pool and play video games. So this seemed to be a good idea at the time.

Now, before I go any further, there are a few things you need to know.

- John Herschel Lill III is stubborn. If he thinks that he is right or thinks that he can do something, there is no changing his mind.
- In 1978, John Lill and I were two of the scrawniest and unimposing figures into which you could ever run. Back then, we were (and probably still are) horrible fighters and neither of us could run a lick. I weighed only 160 pounds or so and I was the bigger of the two of us.
- When he was a kid, John Lill was not scared of anything, but he should have been. I, on the other hand, while not a complete chicken, possessed a keen *sense of judgment* when it came to saving my own neck.

Now, let's resume the story.

John Lill and I strolled into the Fair Play Game Room on that Saturday night in '78 with no real plans or worries. We picked out a pool table, put in a quarter, and started to play. We had played only a game or two when the door opened and in walked five or six regulars. They were about our age and were loud and laughing among themselves. As John and I continued with our game, the six locals started playing video games and eventually gravitated over toward the pool tables and us.

As they got closer, I could hear a couple of the local boys jawing about us being on their "regular table." At first, I paid no attention to it, but it got louder, and a whiff of beer was then in the air. This caused the little computer in my head to begin to calculate our options and the only one I could come up with that did not include me bleeding was to simply finish our game and leave.

I leaned over and shared my feelings with John, and he sharply (and loudly) replied, "NO, we were here first!" I then told John I was sure the six locals didn't care about the evening's order of arrival. He again was defiant, saying, "We can take care of ourselves!" When he said that, I looked over my shoulder for the rest of "we." I was disappointed to find my memory was correct, and that the "we" John spoke of was only the two of us. John then began to jaw right back at them.

By the time I told one of the locals that we'd swap tables with them, it was too late. John and their *spokes-drunk* had used up all the goodwill in that little shack. In a last desperate attempt to save our necks, I started nudging John toward the door. By the time I got him into the parking lot and then into the truck, several of our *new friends* had made it outside, too. As I drove off, John Herschel Lill III was hanging out the window of the truck, still yelling at those boys. He was relentless.

Once we were a mile or two down the road and clear of our troubles, I asked John, "What the hell were you thinking back there?" He told me that he thought we could have held our own. I then informed him he had thought wrong, because my six buddies and I would have killed him.

Over the 55-plus years we can remember knowing each other, my friendship with John Lill has never wavered. He remains one of my closest and dearest friends—and he's also my accountant, which worries me to no end.

* * *

The Tree Climbing Story

When I was a kid, one of the biggest days of the year was the first day of baseball practice. The first day of practice in the spring of 1973 was no different. Weeks of anticipation had led up to the Saturday when **Frankie Nunn** was going to take his Masonic Lodge Team onto the field for its first workouts of the year.

My buddy John Ruark and I had spent the better part of the morning prior to our first practice of 1973 killing time by busting up a beaver dam on a creek that sat behind his Uncle Parnell's place. (I must admit, I never knew why we had to bring that dam down, but John was positive it had to go, so we did it.) After we finished with demolishing the dam, we went for lunch. Afterwards, we got on his Honda ATC 90 and made our way towards town for baseball practice. Now this is where the story really begins.

For reasons I cannot recall (you'll discover why later), we made our way down to Bostwick and somehow met up with Gene Knight and his cousin Joey. The two of them were in town for baseball practice, too. It was not common for John and me to see Gene and Joey a lot. I guess it was because Gene lived out towards Fairplay (Georgia) and Joey lived in Fairplay. (Once the four of us were together, the main characters were all in place for an occurrence I'll never live down.)

Some way, somehow, the four of us made it to the Methodist preacher's (**Benny Harmon**) house. In the front yard of the Methodist parsonage was, and remains, a large magnolia tree. It has big limbs that are low to the ground and was easy pickings for climbing.

We had an hour or so before baseball practice, so John and I decided to climb the tree. I guess we were still feeling bold after bringing those beavers to their knees earlier in the day. Up we went, higher and higher. Neither of us was willing (smart enough) to stop and we both eventually reached the tiptop of that magnolia. Gene and Joey remained on the ground and kidded us as we ascended. At one point while we were near the top, one of them mocked the great comedian Jerry Clower and yelled, "Whooooo, knock him out John." *As you continue reading, remember that.* Then we started down.

Now at this point, I must confess that I am writing without first-hand memory and am relying on John's recollection.

Apparently, as we started down, I failed to heed John's advice to, "Watch that rotten limb." He tells me I argued with him and insisted the limb would hold me. If that is so, I was wrong. Evidently, I stepped on that "rotten" limb. Then, from approximately 25 feet off the ground, I became a human pinball. My 100-pound (soaking wet) body clanked, clunked, flopped, and bounced off every limb that tree had. Let's just say, I easily beat John to the ground. I slammed to Earth with a thud and all the breath flew from my unconscious body.

As I lay there, out like a light, Joey, who was a big boy, ran over and easily lifted me up into his arms. Here's where the story gets real funny for everybody but me.

While Joey was standing there, holding me, Gene screamed out, "He's dead!" Joey then dropped me—thump! Folks, I had just fallen 25 feet from a tree, knocked myself silly and Joey Knight picked me up and then immediately dropped me. There's life in a nutshell.

I don't know who, but one of them then ran and got Mrs. Harmon, who came out with a wet rag trying to bring me around. By then, they had found Gene's initial diagnosis to be wrong. I was actually still alive. Mrs. Harmon started to rouse me a bit, and I eventually rose up, at which time I vomited all over the Methodist preacher's wife.

During all of this, someone had called my house and got my grandmother. She in turn called my **Uncle Felton (Knight)**. The two of them got into a car and rushed to the scene. By the time they arrived, I was conscious enough to be sitting there crying. My insides felt like melted Jell-O, my head hurt, and I wasn't sure where I was.

From here on, I am back using my own memory.

Joined by my mother, Granny and Uncle Felton sped me to the hospital where Dr. McGeary met us. He X-rayed me and checked me over. He determined I had two broken ribs, a concussion, and some internal bruises. Due to the concussion, I was forced to spend the night in the hospital. Now, one would think that would have been pretty much it for my troubles that day. Oh no.

Fairly soon after I got into my hospital room, in walked my Pa-Pa, and he was crying his eyes out. Now, his sobbing was probably an even split of: 1) his genuine concern for me, and 2) whatever he'd been drinking that afternoon while I was busy falling out of that tree. So, in walked a blubbering Pa-Pa. He proceeded to walk right over to my bed, lean over and give me a huge hug, while he continued to squall. He was carrying on so much about my health that he could not hear everybody in the room telling him that it was not a "good idea" to give people with internal bleeding "big hugs."

Well, I started crying because Pa-Pa was scaring and killing me. Granny started fussing at him and my Ma-Ma started crying, but no one seemed to try to get him off me. They finally calmed him enough to make him realize he wasn't helping a whole lot. Then, everybody else calmed down, too. Early the next morning, I got to go home. For about a week I was sore from head to toe. Breathing was extremely painful for a month.

I learned something that day about John Ruark that I have

kept with me over the years. You can say what you'd like about him, but I tell you this about John Ruark: He knows a *rotten limb* when he sees one.

Through our 55+ years of living, John Ruark and I have always been there for each other. He remains one of my closest friends. We talk often, still go to races when we can, and no longer climb trees.

2

PA-PA

Bostwick is a modest place with wonderful people. When I was growing up there in the '60s and '70s its population struggled to reach 300. Today its citizenship numbers a whopping 375 or so. It was the kind of place where the men, who labored Monday through Saturday and went to church on Sundays, had to sneak off to *take a drink* and they called every lady in town "Miss."

I was influenced by several of these gentlemen. There was Mr. George Lee Ruark whose grandson, John, remains one of my closest friends. Mr. Hammond Calloway was a leader in our church. When he prayed on Sundays it sounded as he was having a one-on-one conversation with God. Then there was the primary male influence of my childhood, for that matter my whole life—Mr. Robert C. Whitlock Sr. (Pa-Pa).

My grandfather was a *character*—plain and simple. He had a personality so complex that if Sigmund Freud had attempted to analyze it, he would have given up, but he would have loved my Pa-Pa—nearly everyone did. Pa-Pa was the kind of man that would cuss you out for not closing your eyes while he said the blessing with his eyes wide open.

Pa-Pa, Granny, and Me when I was 4 in 1965

Due to circumstances not uncommon to the South during my childhood, I was raised primarily by my grandparents. As the oldest of their four grandchildren, I was "Pa-Pa's favorite" (if you don't believe me, ask my sister). From the day I was born he showed special interest in me. If I wanted it, Pa-Pa got it for me. I was his shadow and he was a giant to me. My grandfather had little formal education but possessed great instincts. If he liked you, you had an ally that would kill for you. If he didn't like you, or if you crossed him, he was a huge pain in your ass.

During my entire early life, he saw to it that my siblings and I were clothed, fed, educated, and cared for. He taught me the value of an honest day's work. He also showed me the *consequences* of not doing "your day's work." He loved his family. He adored (and was quite afraid of) his wife, my grandmother, Mozelle.

There are limitless stories I could share about my grandfather. There is the one where he sat in the back of the auditorium at Piedmont College and cried while I graduated—becoming first in our family to graduate from college. There's the story of how at age 72 (and I was 23) he assured me he could still "kick my skinny ass"—and I believed him! But, the one story I'd like to share with you about my grandfather is the one that involved our final telephone conversation.

In the autumn of 1987, I was married, working at Kennesaw State, and living in Marietta (some 85 miles from Bostwick). I always looked forward to going home where I would get a chance to visit my buddies and my grandparents. During my visits home there would seemingly always be a point where Pa-Pa and I would get away and talk. He'd tell me about how Granny was spending too much money or how the Republican Party was ruining Western civilization. In turn, I'd whine about my wife and being broke—at that point he'd usually slip me some money. I cherished every second of those talks. I'd give anything if I could have just one more talk with him. Here's why:

When I got married in September of 1984, I went home every time I had a few free hours, but as time went along my trips home went from weekly, to every couple of weeks, to monthly. This bothered my grandfather. He did not understand why my life was so hectic that I couldn't get home. No matter my rationale he was always heartbroken when I went a couple of weeks without getting home. It was one of the few issues we never settled. Today, I deeply regret that.

On Saturday, September 12, 1987, I had my final telephone conversation with my grandfather. He called that morning and wanted to know if we were coming for lunch on Sunday. I told him "no" that we couldn't come because "I had too much going on, but maybe next week."

What I had going on was that I wanted to watch a stock car race and a football game on TV. In other words, I just did not want to go home on that particular weekend! I made a choice, I could have gone. I chose, however, not to go visit with the two people that had worked every day to give me a better life than they had. In my mind that was fine because I was going to go next week.

We talked a bit longer, I tried to make him feel better, but I hung up with him unhappy with me. Now, that happened before—we would fight or fuss, but we would always work through it and settle things. The disagreement during the call of the 12th was never to be settled.

I did not speak to anyone back home on Sunday. On Monday (September 14th) I went to work. We were in meetings. They were long and boring. That afternoon there was a reception and party for staff as well as faculty. My buddies and I had a blast at the party. I had a great afternoon laughing and talking —this was a time prior to the age of cell phones and email, so there was no way that anything could interrupt our party and my fun.

I took my time getting home. My wife worked nights, so I was in no rush. Once I did get home, I went through my paces. I fed the dog, got the mail, and changed clothes. Finally, I got around to checking our answering machine. When I punched the machine, I received a message from my brother Phillip, "Scott, call Granny. Pa-Pa's been in a wreck and is in the hospital. I think he's OK, but you need to call home." I quickly dialed. As I did, I thought to myself, "Wonder what he hit this time?" He was no stranger to fender benders. I wondered if he had sneaked off for a bit of bourbon and ran into a ditch. I thought, "Boy, he's going to catch hell from Granny." When the phone was answered at their home, it was not Granny on the line. It was my aunt. "Joyce, this is Scott where's Granny? I just got home and got Phil's message. How's Pa-Pa doing?" There was a long sickening pause. I knew then what was about to be said. Aunt Joyce replied to me, "Oh Scotty, you haven't heard? He's gone." My heart shattered. I'm sure she said more, but I honestly do not remember anything else. I think I spoke with

Granny but I'm not sure. All I could think about were the words "He's gone!"

The days that followed are also a blur. The only steadfast memory that I have of those days is my guilt. To this day, I still cannot believe that I was so neglectful with the relationship that existed between my grandfather and me. He had been the center of my world for nearly all of my life and I let a car race and football game keep me from seeing him the day before he died!

Now I realize we can't see into the future and I'm not the first to experience such guilt. However, since the 14th of September in 1987, I have always felt a bit lonely. My best friend is gone, and I'll never get to see him again on this Earth.

I urge everyone to tell anyone that's important to you just how you feel and to never miss an opportunity to go visit your parents, grandparents, loved ones, or anyone else who has shaped your life. You see, there is no guarantee of next week.

Trust me on this one.

Now THAT's my Pa-Pa

3

DON MCKINLAY AND ME

There is absolutely no way I could write about my career (or life) without including an account of my relationship with Don McKinlay. For 13 years, we worked in tandem building the KSU softball program. My friend Mike Candrea has opened more doors for me than anyone in our business. However, it was Don who was there with me in my early days and it was from him that I learned much of what I know about teaching the fundamentals of our game. Next to Coach Candrea, Don is the best one-on-one instructor with whom I have ever worked. I have so many stories I could share about Don and me, so let's start from the beginning.

In the late 1980s, my life was on cruise control. I was working as an assistant to Ron Walker with Kennesaw State's women's basketball team (we were great together, Ron had the best basketball mind I had ever been around, and I was fairly useless) and our slowpitch softball team was dominant. With me working for a great coach like Ron and running an outstanding softball team like the KSU teams of the late '80s, I had a fairly easy gig. That changed during a meeting that I attended one morning in the winter of 1988. I was called to my boss's office—Dr. Dave Waples who was the AD at Kennesaw State for over 20 years.

* * *

Coach Waples became—*what was then*—Kennesaw College's athletic director when Coach Spec Landrum retired in the spring of 1987. Over the 24 years Waples and I worked together, we witnessed enormous change at Kennesaw State. We saw a *college* of 5,500 grow to become a *university* of more than 25,000. We also saw a fledgling athletic department grow into a prolific intercollegiate athletic program that can now boast several national championships and too many conference titles to mention while enjoying unprecedented *balance*. What I mean by balance is fairness, consistency, and integrity.

Small college and *mid-major* athletic directors' decisions on budgets usually set the course an athletic department will take. There are no big-time, high-roller boosters behind the scenes calling the shots. So, who gets the *juice* is generally left up to the AD. Some chose to dump the majority of the budget into one or two sports—usually men's and women's basketball and/or football—leaving the other sports to fend for themselves. Waples never opted for that. Since the day he arrived, no coach of a sport at KSU could place the blame of failure on lack of funding or resources. Each coach was given a chance to win. As a coach of what is perceived as a *minor sport* in many eyes, I will always be grateful to Dave Waples for that.

* * *

As I said, in early 1988 I was called into Coach Waples' office for a meeting. When I sat down and listened to one of Coach Waples' stories' (one never went into his office without having the pleasure of hearing a story or listening to him tell you why he's giving up golf), this was our conversation:

> Waples: "Scott what do you know about fastpitch softball?"
>
> Me: "Nothing. I've never seen it played."
>
> Waples: "What do you think about us converting our softball team to it?"
>
> Me: "That would be stupid. No one down here plays it; we'd have no recruiting base. I think that it is foolish to give up a sport in which we are so dominant for a sport we know nothing about."
>
> Waples: "Well, we are going to move to fastpitch in the fall of 1990. So, if you want to coach here, you better embrace it and start learning."
>
> Me: "I've always said, fastpitch is the wave of the future. Boss, it's a shrewd move on your part to turn me loose with that sport."

That's how I become a fastpitch coach.

* * *

Now, what's all that got to do with Don McKinlay? The answer is—*plenty*. Once given the chore of becoming a fastpitch coach, I started studying anything I could in order to prepare myself. In my preparation, I quickly decided the things that I *could not* do.

I am very much aware of what I can and cannot do—always have been. Maybe it's because there is so much at which I am incompetent. My willingness to admit my limits is one of the best personal traits that I ever employed over my career. I have never had any problem with hiring others to compensate for my weaknesses. A lot of coaches (especially young ones) hesitate to confess their deficiencies. I never did. Somehow, I knew it was OK for others to know more about certain aspects of the game than me. I also knew if we were going to ever be any good, someone other than me would have to teach the mechanics of pitching and hitting.

My baseball background gave me a good fundamental foundation from which to build and teach, but I knew I was not qualified to teach the mechanics of pitching and I was certain that I'd be *very limited* as a hitting coach. It was clear that my assistants would have to have those skill sets.

Back in those days there was very little, if any, money for assistant coaches at Kennesaw State. A head coach had to be creative as to how to get assistants. This is where Don and my paths cross.

Late in May of 1988, I traveled to Jacksonville, Florida, to watch our baseball team play in an NAIA Regional Tournament. We have always had great baseball at KSU and the 1988 season was one of the best. My slowpitch season was over and I was down there to relax and enjoy some baseball.

As the week unfolded, I began to notice the swing of one of our two senior catchers. I thought to myself, "This kid's swing is sweet." Of course, the player I am referring to was Don McKinlay. Don enjoyed a great tournament. He was as hot as any hitter could be. His team finished second to a fine North Florida team that week.

For reasons I cannot remember, I was asked by our then-baseball coach Chip Reese to drive their team bus home (I think his family had come down and he wanted to ride home with them). Anyway, at dinner that night, by sheer coincidence, I sat across from Don. I had seen him at school of course, but we had never officially met. We had a great chat. I congratulated him on a great tournament and was impressed by his respectful demeanor.

I learned he was Canadian, a native of Lethbridge, Alberta.

I also found out he had changed his major from business to education and was facing a couple extra years of college. It was then that the best idea of my career was born.

I thought to myself, "I wonder if this kid can teach softball players how to swing a bat like he does?" At that point, we finished dinner, loaded the bus, and headed north.

The drive from Jacksonville back to Kennesaw usually takes about six hours, but that night I had a good *tailwind* and we made it in about five (*still a school record*). At some point during the drive home, I called Don up to the front of the bus and asked him to have a seat on the cooler beside me. I re-engaged in talking to him about his future. He said that he was going to stay at Kennesaw and continue school. When I asked him about his work situation, he said he had nothing lined up, but he was going to be looking.

Then, I sprung it on him. "Have you ever thought about coaching women?" He quickly said, "No." Then I went into detail regarding what was about to take place with the softball program. He began to take an interest, and somewhere between Valdosta and Macon on I-75, Don McKinlay was hired as my assistant coach. He has been by my side either literally or figuratively ever since.

We spent the 1989-90 school year coaching Kennesaw State's final slowpitch team and preparing for the big transition. One of our first jobs was to *find pitching*. It was during our search that Don made an immediate (and the most important) impact on the history of KSU softball. Don recalled that one of his former teammates back in Alberta had a sister who pitched. That guy's sister turned out to be Kennesaw State Athletic Hall of Famer—Dyan Mueller (see chapter 15).

Our first two years together in fastpitch were as much fun as I have ever had playing or coaching. Neither of us had a clue as to what we were doing, and no one expected much from us.

What freedom and what an advantage! It was apparent from the beginning that we complimented each other famously.

Don is a shy, usually calm individual. I am more like *Barney Fife* with a softball bat. Don is methodical and patient. I am like a golf ball hit inside a phone booth. Don shuns the spotlights and hates to speak in public. I am a ham. Don is a *good cop* coach. I am...well, let's just say that as a coach I am more like a *Dirty Harry*.

There were other things apparent about Don at the onset and each attribute is still present today.

- He has a great eye for talent.
- Don was born to coach female athletes. His rapport with our players and his students is something to strive for.
- He is a great technician; there are few better.
- He has great patience (if you don't believe that, you try working for me for 13 years).
- He works harder than anyone I know.
- His genuine concern for people is rivaled only by his loyalty to those whom he is close.

Our *rhythm* was there from the start. We decided to build the fastpitch program based on what we knew, learn on the fly, and not be scared. It worked. With Don smoothing the waters behind me and my continued pushing an inexperienced group to overachieve, our first team won 41 games and posted a fourth-place national finish (NAIA). The rest is history.

In the 11 seasons that followed, we never failed to make the national tournament and we advanced to the final round of eight in 10 of those seasons. We claimed two national championships (1995 & 1996) and had more than 30 players receive All-America honors. If I was the program's *head*, Don surely was its *spine*. He was always there for the players (as well as the head coach). In all the years we were together, I never saw him have a bad day at practice or be impolite to anyone.

Don retired from collegiate coaching at the end of the 2002 season. Today he is one of Atlanta's busiest hitting instructors. He also owns part interest in a softball equipment retail business. He, his lovely wife Cindy, and their two kids still live in Kennesaw. We talk regularly and see each other when we can.

I still lean on him for advice. To refer to Don McKinlay as my friend would be *shortchanging* my regard for him. He is my brother. I am so proud of him.

While we were together, the Kennesaw State softball program had the highest winning percentage in the history of collegiate softball (.877) and much of that was due to Don's calm reassuring nature, his skills as a coach, and his friendship. I say without hesitation, if it were not for Don McKinlay, no one would have ever heard of Scott Whitlock.

Thanks for the career—and being my brother, Donny.

Enjoying a KSU football game with Don (left) in 2018

4

THE KING AND I

Very few people can honestly say that their professional hero is also one of their best friends. I can. Many people in my business have met Coach Mike Candrea, watched him coach, or heard him speak. Very few are allowed personal access. I am.

As to the following assessment, I am very biased, and I offer no apologies.

John Michael Candrea *is the BEST coach and teacher in the history of the sport of softball.* I did not say, *among the..., one of the ..., or might be the...he is the BEST ever*—end of story! He has been the head softball coach at the University of Arizona for more than 30 years. He has won eight national championships and has led the USA to an Olympic gold medal. In his field of expertise, there is Candrea, and then there is the discussion as to who is second best. Now we can move on.

Our first official meeting was in New Orleans, during one of the most terrifying two hours of my life (see chapter 21). On that day, either I impressed Mike Candrea, or he pitied me, because since NOLA, he has always made time or a place for me.

After our meeting, I made the jump from *acquaintance* to

employee and then to *family* seemingly in a matter of months. For over two decades, I have counted our friendship and bond among my most prized possessions. Strange though, despite our close friendship, I cannot think of a single time that I have benefited professionally by being associated with Mike Candrea. *That is if you do not count*:

- Taking a chance on me 20 years ago by putting me on stage—*leading to countless speaking opportunities for me all over North America*
- Hiring me (*and overpaying me*) to work at his camps and clinics for more than 20 years
- Helping me attain and keep endorsement opportunities
- Allowing me to be a part of two Olympic cycles
- Traveling all over the world with him
- Introducing me to great recruiting contacts
- Playing golf with him at exclusive courses
- Being his dinner companion at great Italian restaurants

Wait, the above statement is not completely true. **I will admit that I did whine (and whine) until he consented to write the foreword for this book.** Therefore, I guess—*if you want to get nitpicky about it*—one could say that our friendship did benefit me professionally—*as an author*.

All jokes aside, Mike Candrea is a most generous giant. He has helped scores of coaches either get jobs or become better coaches where they are. He has truly given back to his profession. In my case, so much of my professional reputation and success has come about from his kindness. Getting his endorsement early on opened many doors for me. There is no doubt that my career would look vastly different if it were not for him. I will be forever grateful.

When people in our profession bring up Mike Candrea, his amazing record and coaching skills are usually at the hub of the conversation. When they bring him up to me, my first thoughts are *respect* and *genuine friendship*. Those attributes are what stand out in my mind when the Italian gentleman from the desert is mentioned in my presence. He is part of my family and I am a part of his.

* * *

Acceptance

From day one, he has always accepted me for who I am, and I reciprocate. When we work together, I do not attempt to impress him by trying to be a clone or imitate him. I just go out and do my thing and it works. He has always liked that about me. I have never tried to be anyone other than myself. I cannot teach like Mike. *He's "The King" and teaches softball at the highest of levels. Hell, I do not even understand most of it.*

By the way, he hates that nickname. For all his success, he is quite humble and private. He does not like attention. Anyway...

I would be a fool to go out in front of kids or coaches and try to teach in the same manner as he. So, I present as an *everyman* type of coach—because that is what I am.

When trying to tell clinic attendees about what to expect from Coach Candrea and me, I say, "Coach Candrea is the greatest teacher that our game has ever known, and I am his opening act." It is kind of like Don Rickles opening for Frank Sinatra—and we are both fine with that.

In all professions (and in life), too many people make the mistake of trying to *compete* with or imitate greatness. I never have. I am just happy to have the chance to listen and learn from it. I know who I am. I am not a hitting coach or great technician, and that is OK with me. I feel that a person limits their productivity when they try to be someone they are not. I have made a good living being fully aware of what I cannot do.

When having a chance to hear someone as accomplished as a Candrea speak about his/her field, many miss chances to learn because they become insecure upon realizing they are no longer *the smartest person in the room.* They would be better off to check their egos at the door and be willing to learn. Fortunately, I have never had that problem. Working with Candrea all these years, I never have to deal with that kind of stuff —*because he will be the first to tell anyone that I am never the smartest one in the room.* What a pal! I recall the word "limited" quickly being used when I once asked him for a critique of my skill set. Yes sir, what a pal!

The King and I

Laughter

As you might guess, laughter is at the center of our friendship. Laughing and enjoying time with friends are important to John Michael Candrea. It is important to me, too. Therefore, for me the math is simple: I can make Mike Candrea laugh, therefore he puts up with me. In addition, *when he chooses,* he can make me nervous and having that ability makes him laugh—*so*

I have that going for me, which is nice. I have learned that a laughing King is a happy King.

Regarding his ability to make me nervous: In just about any setting, Mike can say or do something to me and I will become *Barney Fife trying to load his pistol.* He found that he could do that to me early in our friendship and he holds it over me. There are many stories about that (you can read about the origin of this spell in chapter 21) and he uses it. He knows exactly how to push the nerve button on Scott Whitlock.

Mike Candrea's camp staff has been made up of the same core of five people for nearly 20 years. There is Mike, his older brother Nick, Dave "Bull" Moore, Jav Vela, and myself. We are a close-knit group, and love to laugh together—and no one is immune from a good roasting.

As I mentioned, I am someone who can make Mike Candrea laugh. He likes to hear me tell stories (*some of them over and over*), and he especially loves to watch me when I needle his brother Nick or verbally spar with Jav. Some of the best times of my life have been when we are in his living room, on his patio, or in a restaurant. He will give me a look and then nod at either Nick or Jav. That is his way of signaling, "Go get him!" Then we are off to the races. The madder I can make one of them, the harder he laughs. The more they return fire, the more everyone laughs. Those are special moments.

Tina

I feel it is proper at this point, to mention Mrs. John Michael Candrea, Tina. She is a very kind and understanding soul. Jav and I were with Mike when he met Tina, we were at their wedding, and we are so happy they found each other. They are a great match.

When the camp crew descends upon Tucson, Arizona, Tina

becomes the *house mom* of a very unpredictable fraternity. Throughout each visit, she holds the crew in check, and makes us all feel welcome in their home. *She always has my Oreos and Coca-Colas—so she will always be aces in my book.*

* * *

Trust and Loyalty

Another reason our friendship works is due to the absolute trust we have for each other. For some reason, this has always been a given between us. Loyalty is a requisite to be welcomed within Coach Candrea's orbit. John Michael knows he can count on me and that I will never embarrass his reputation. He knows that I can open for him at a clinic by entertaining and teaching the attendees—*sometimes by kidding him about his accomplishments and place in our sport*, and he never has to worry about me being prepared to work or going overboard. He also knows that I view his family as part of my family and I will be protective if necessary.

* * *

Endurance

Real friendships withstand the tests of time and trials. We have stood by one another through thick and thin. It is important to know you have friends like that.

* * *

To wrap this chapter up, the greatest softball coach ever was born in New York, raised in New Orleans, and has lived in the Arizona desert. I am from Bostwick, Georgia, and now reside in Marietta, Georgia. He loves Frank Sinatra, good red wine, delicious Italian food, and the New York Yankees. I like Hank

Williams, Cokes, pork barbecue and Brunswick stew, and my Braves. Though we are very different, it works. We can go weeks without speaking to each other (*he kind of likes that—once he even put me on a "fax-only" basis—thank goodness Tina will take my calls*), but today if the phone would ring and one of us needed the other to get wherever they are, it would happen. It's cool having a friend like that.

It is even cooler when that friend is also one of your heroes. Thanks for everything, King.

5

JAV

My friend Javier "Jav" Vela of Tomball, Texas, is difficult to explain. At a quick glance, one is likely to view him as a rowdy, boisterous, and near uncontrollable wild man. They would be right. With a closer look, you would find an intelligent, funny, caring, and talented man.

Jav grew up poor and a hard worker on the USA side of the Texas-Mexico border in the 1950s. He went on to attend and play football at Texas A&M, where he played on the 1968 Cotton Bowl championship team. In that game, his Aggies defeated Bear Bryant's Crimson Tide—something in which he still takes great pride. During his life, Jav has been a farmer, stockbroker, teacher, and coach.

During his coaching career he has won a state high school softball championship, coached a professional softball team, taught countless kids to hit and/or pitch, and earned a spot working at camps and clinics for the greatest softball coach ever—which is where our paths first crossed.

I first met Jav in 1996 in Tucson, Arizona. It was my first of many trips to that town. I was there to speak at Mike Candrea's annual coaching clinic.

Me with The King and Jav

On the afternoon before the clinic began, I was visiting with Coach Candrea in his office when this large, rubber-faced fellow exploded into the room. No knock, no peek-in, no nothing. He just pounced upon us like a panther. And, while wearing a huge smile, he demanded a hat and requested that Coach give him the keys to the softball equipment room immediately. When Coach flatly denied the request, the guy flew into an uncontrollable, cursing rage and stomped out.

The exchange slightly frightened me. After all, this was my first time working for Coach Candrea and I really didn't know what to expect. But I knew what I just witnessed could not be normal. "What was that?" I asked. And, without missing a beat, Mike chuckled and replied, "That's just Jav."

At the time, I felt his answer was extremely vague, but after now knowing Jav for more than two decades, I totally understand. You see, I have come to know that Jav can only be described with one word—Jav. There are no other words that can describe him. He's just Jav.

Jav's voice is unique. His mannerisms are definitely his own. And he even looks differently than anyone else. He's just Jav.

During the remainder of that particular trip to Tucson, Jav and I spoke very little. We weren't even formally introduced. However, I do recall him making some joke about me being a bit "rural." Other than that, not much else happened.

As time went along, and as I worked more regularly for Coach Candrea, I saw more and more of Jav. And as we spent time around each other, Jav and I became friends—good friends.

Our friendship has a certain rhythm to it. We know our roles within it, and we enjoy that we have a lot in common. We take great pleasure in making fun of each other and the world.

To be a stranger and hear us talking, you would think that Jav and I are about to kill each other. The references we use toward each other in one of our debates make some, in today's PC-crazed world, very uncomfortable. That matters very little to us because we get it. People who know us (and what we are doing) *get it.* We understand and trust each other. We both love to joke, laugh, and jab at (and are jabbed by) people—and, we especially love to hassle each other. No one can make me laugh any harder than Jav Vela.

One of our specialties is *holding court.* Whether it is at a soft-ball camp after work, between sessions at a clinic, in a restaurant, or in Coach Candrea's living room, Jav and I love it when a crowd gathers to witness one of our *discussions.* It matters very little who's actually right or wrong about an issue. If truth be told, *we nearly always agree,* but that does not deter the act. We just love to argue. When a crowd gathers, if he say's "white," I say "black" and away we go. We'll argue over nothing, or everything, for 10 minutes and have everybody rolling (especially ourselves).

Here's how it goes: I usually am the agitating straight man and Jav is the frustrated comic. I say something that will seemingly make him furious and we're off to the races. His face changes shape, his hands get busy as he rants without pause, and he looks as if he's about to kill me.

In fact, Coach Candrea has said to me many times, "One of these days he's going to snap and kill you." Coach's tone is always a bit hopeful when he says this, but much to his disappointment, Jav never snaps and attacks.

After we banter for a few minutes, it usually ends by him stomping out, pretending to be mad, and leaving the room to smoke a cigarette—always outside.

Everyone should have friends with whom he/she can be comfortable just being crazy. I guess Jav is one of mine. He is also one of the few people in which I know that I can truly rely. Jav Vela is a good man. I would never tell him that. That's not our style.

When I decided to write this book, I knew I had to write a chapter on Jav. He's too big a part of my story to omit. After struggling to single out a story or two, I have settled on how I wish to pay tribute to my dear friend.

I am going to share with you the letter I wrote to be read at Jav's retirement tribute—when he concluded a legendary run as Klein Oak High School's (Spring, Texas) softball coach.

So, with apologies for a few redundancies, I would like to share my friend Javier Vela with the world.

* * *

"Somebody help me get out of Louisiana, just help me get to Houston town; there are people there that care a little 'bout me and they won't let the po' boy down."

— CHUCK BERRY (AS SUNG BY ELVIS PRESLEY)

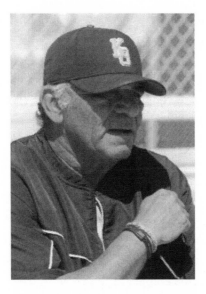

Jav

April 17, 2015

Greetings to All:

At this letter's onset, I want to tell everyone just how much I wanted to be present for this celebration, but circumstances would not allow it.

I first met Coach Vela over 20 years ago. I was sitting in Mike Candrea's office when a steamroller of a man (who possessed unique facial contours and a distinctive speaking voice) came barging into the room demanding keys. When Coach Candrea denied the request, the man cussed and stomped out. I quickly asked Coach, "Who was that?" His response consisted of only one word—"JAV." Though I did not know it then, I now realize that I had just heard the definitive description of Coach Javier Vela. JAV— that says it all. That one word description is as unique and indisputable as the man that wears it—"JAV." I know of no one else who can be so perfectly described with just a single syllable—JAV. There are no other words that would be appropriate. He WAS, IS, and ALWAYS will BE JAV. Even now, two decades later, if I speak of the man when telling stories, people will occasionally ask me questions. Things like, "Describe him for me." I reply, "He's JAV." "What does he look like?" I say, "He looks like JAV." "To whom can you compare him?" "NO ONE—he's JAV."

Happenstance threw us together and we soon became members of the summer camp staff for the legendary Candrea —the chemistry between Jav and I was near instant and irrefutable.

It quickly became clear that our roles within the camp company were two-fold, yet quite simple. Our jobs were to 1) share our softball knowledge with campers during the day, and 2) make "The King" laugh at night. That has never changed— we teach, then we argue; we teach, then we argue; and so it goes.

When someone who does not know us experiences our act for the first time, their immediate thought is usually, "These guys are crazy." Then they think, "Hey, these two nuts are about to kill each other—or someone else." Then they see that it's all an act.

Everyone who encounters us quickly realizes that we are just two guys who love life and love to laugh at it. They quickly sense our genuine affection and regard for each other. And anyone who is willing to can quickly see that both of us love people—it's just that neither of us can fully understand why some people choose to take themselves so seriously. Life is just too short.

Make no mistake, we both take our profession seriously. But luckily, we were never infected with the disease of *self-importance*. We have both enjoyed great success as coaches, our records speak for themselves, but it is our ability to laugh and *enjoy the ride* that define us. I am so glad we were both born immune to arrogance and egotism. I treasure the times I have spent with Jav laughing at life and just being ourselves.

We have seen each other in some funny situations. Jav was with me when I hit a church van with the camp's equipment truck in a McDonald's parking lot and I was there to witness his near heart attack when Candrea talked him into staying in a $300 poker pot (which he eventually won).

Of the scores of escapades that we have shared, *many of which will never be rehashed*, none means more to me than the six days in July of 2004 when we stood beside a brother as he dealt with the tragic loss of his wife. I'll never forget how each night, in the midst of great tragedy, a family and their friends would gravitate to a living room in Casa Grande, Arizona, to listen to Jav and I *hold court*. Though I didn't know it at the time, upon reflection, I believe our nightly antics were our way of reminding our brother that we loved him, and he was not alone. For just a couple of minutes each night of that horrible week, we made a family laugh—easing their pain during the darkest of times. It was perhaps the most decent and humane thing either of us will ever do.

And so, here in April of 2015, we celebrate the coaching legacy of Coach Jav Vela at Klein Oak High School.

Sometime ago I read for every life a person touches in a positive manner, the number of additional lives that are positively influenced can multiply by over 100-fold. Applying that notion, and using my marginal skills in mathematical theory, I calculated it could be argued that *my friend* Jav has enriched the lives of well over 100,000 people over the course of his Klein Oak career. Most of that number could, of course, be traced back to the student-athletes, assistant coaches, parents, and peers here; but on this day, I want everyone in attendance to know that Jav Vela's positive influence is not exclusive to metropolitan Houston or the state of Texas.

For two decades, I have observed him work with young people in camp settings across the country. I have seen him masterfully employ his unique style while teaching the sport of softball. I have witnessed him make kids better players; I have seen him instill needed confidence and self-esteem into many youngsters. I have even seen him make a homesick kid laugh. His work has touched so many. **Coach Jav Vela is a role model!**

As I end this letter, I want you to publicly thank my brother, **Coach Jav Vela** for the positive influence he has on my life. I am a richer person for having him in my world; and, I want to congratulate him for having such a great career at Klein Oak. *Salud*, my dear friend and brother. I love you.

Scott

Well folks, that's JAV. Please don't tell him that I love him.

6

BROTHER FROM ANOTHER MOTHER

Sunday, April 2, 2017, was a horrible, life-changing day. My brother from another mother, Warren "Rhubarb" Jones died. He was 65. While waiting to have a car battery installed at a local Walmart, he slumped over in a chair —GONE from a massive heart attack. A man who had the knack of making noise wherever he was left suddenly and quietly. I may never fully recover from the shock.

I realize that death comes with living. I am aware Rhubarb was overweight and did not take good care of himself, but the suddenness of his leaving caught me totally unprepared. Rhubarb Jones had a particular set of jobs within my life and I now find him unavailable. His unexpected departure left me without having a Rhubarb understudy waiting in the wings. As I write this three months later, I'm still at a loss.

* * *

Before I go any further, I want to be clear that this chapter is not an effort to deify Rhubarb Jones. Rhubarb was a complex and flawed person to say the least. He lived a complicated life.

His soul was splotched with scars—many from self-inflicted wounds; but that is not what this chapter is about. The following words are about the Rhubarb I knew and our friendship. The chapter also serves, on some levels, as catharsis for a grieving brother.

* * *

Rhubarb and I were, for each other, *the guy* that the other one could call to make them laugh or feel better in any dark moment. This happened often as we tried to make it through this world. We could rely on each other to ease any sting or hurt—by commiserating or by making the hurting soul laugh. Usually, this involved sprinkling a bit of salt in the fresh wound, or by making a sarcastic comment about the circumstance— but *never* inappropriately.

When you get down to it, we were completely at ease with each other. Rhubarb didn't need one thing from me and I didn't want one thing from him—we both knew it. So, when we were together (or talking on the phone), we were just two old boys (that knew the Good Lord had smiled on us) who spent most of our time laughing at what life throws at you and enjoying each other's company.

I need to backtrack just a bit. I did take advantage of Rhubarb's celebrity once. Had it not been for Rhubarb, I likely would have never had a chance to get my picture taken with George Jones—that was cool.

When experiencing us together for the first time, most left thinking to themselves, "You know...there's something wrong with those boys." But we were having too much fun to care. It was just that simple with Rhuby and me. I hope everyone on Earth has (or finds) someone like that in their life.

Rhuby and I met over 20 years ago—he hated it when most folks called him "Rhuby," but for some reason he granted me a pardon. We first briefly crossed paths at a golf tournament benefiting the Georgia Music Hall of Fame at Chateau Elan in Braselton, Georgia. However, we officially met at a lunch that was arranged so he could meet Kennesaw State University's Baseball Coach Mike Sansing and me. I cannot remember who arranged that lunch, but for more than two decades, I have owed them a heartfelt thank you.

Meeting Rhubarb was easy for me, because I had ridden to work with Jones for years. Rhubarb was a country music radio icon. My mornings usually started with me listening to the various incarnations of his morning show on Atlanta's WYAY 106.7 FM. All his listeners felt as if they knew him personally because he came across so genuine. He was one of us. Rhubarb Jones was a GIANT in country music radio.

* * *

Rhubarb's career as an on-air radio personality began in 1971 at WPID in Piedmont, Alabama, playing gospel music on Sunday afternoons. In 1972, WWCC in Bremen, Georgia, became his radio home until 1974 when he moved to WCLS in Columbus, Georgia, where he played Rock & Roll.

The year 1975 was a pivotal one in the life and career of Rhubarb Jones. It was then that he accepted a job offer from WSKY in Asheville, North Carolina, and it was at WSKY he played and fell in love with country music. After three years in Asheville, it was on to WLWI in Montgomery, Alabama, in 1978 where he did the afternoon drive and served as program and music director for seven years.

In February of 1985, Rhubarb Jones came home when he joined Atlanta's WYAY 106.7. For the following 23 years, he and his compatriots accompanied commuters on their morning drive. It was while at WYAY, the kid from Tallapoosa became a state treasure and a radio icon.

Over his 37+ year radio career, he earned nearly every significant industry award including:

- 1983 - Country Music Association Medium Market "Broadcast Personality of the Year"
- 1983 - Academy of Country Music "Radio Personality of the Year"
- 1987 - Country Music Association Large Market "Broadcast Personality of the Year"
- 1988 - "Country Radio Air Personality of the Year" Large Market from Billboard Radio Awards
- 2001 - Inducted into the Country Music Disc Jockey Hall of Fame

* * *

Folks, Rhubarb did it *all* within his line of work. He was among country music radio's elite. Anyway, back to our first meeting. When we showed up that day for lunch, it was easy for me to meet him. I was not nervous because I felt I was among one of my own kind. I really cannot explain it, but starting at that lunch in Marietta, Georgia (at Sonny's on Hwy 41— just south of the Big Chicken), it was as if we had known each other our entire lives. From that day forward, we maintained a near daily conversation that concluded when I last spoke to him on Saturday, April 1, 2017. Over the two and a half decades we knew each other, we truly grew to be brothers.

One of the cornerstones of our relationship was we knew when the other needed lying to. When I was down, he would always tell me I was a *great coach* and when he was in a funk, I would always tell him he was the *best country music DJ ever*. Like most brothers, there were times we did not see eye to eye on things, but we never stopped loving each other and we never deserted each other. That's why our last conversation will always be so significant to me.

Rhubarb and I had experienced a lengthy stretch of not seeing eye to eye on a particular matter, but by April 1, 2017, it was obvious that our snit had ended and we were back to business as usual. On the 1st we chatted on the phone for 20 minutes about *nothing* (*Seinfeld* references were part of our lexicon). We laughed and talked, just as close friends or brothers do. As the visit wound down, he told me, "I'm emceeing (Mickey) Gilley tonight at Mill Town in Bremen. I'll holler at you later." And, that was that.

The word *complex* does not do justice when explaining Rhubarb Jones

Rhubarb was a complex person to say the least. His life was complicated, and he was scarred. He was a compulsive and (often) an insecure soul, who self-admittedly suffered from a bad case of *only-child syndrome*. Sometimes he made bad choices. He was a ham. Rhubarb was also one of the most generous, giving, and loving people I have ever met. He was as Kris Kristofferson wrote, "a walking contradiction, partly truth, partly fiction—taking every wrong direction on his lonely way back home."

When you really stop and think about it, Rhuby's faults were not so different from all of ours. They just appeared to be bigger because of his larger-than-life personality and public persona. His fame and notoriety made him an easy candidate for both praise and criticism. His virtues, on the other hand, were grand and oh so genuine. He only used his fame and notoriety to make tremendous, positive impacts on the lives of scores of people.

I want everyone to know, Warren "Rhubarb" Jones (warts and all) was one heck of a guy. I have chosen to brush upon Rhubarb's faults in this writing, to make certain everyone knows I am not trying to make him into a saint. He was not, but he was my brother. Many of his virtues are public record, some were simple random acts of kindness. As strong as his pension was for giving to the public as well as his listeners, his generosity was even bigger when it came to his families—both immediate, extended, and friends.

As I eluded to earlier, Warren Jones was one of the most generous, giving, and loving people I have ever known. He eagerly gave of himself for his listeners and the public. Examples of his big heart include:

- He raised millions of dollars for leukemia and lymphoma—a penny at a time, or at his annual charity golf tournament. Though he never openly said it to me, I believe his grandmother's fight with leukemia was what led him to become so involved with the Leukemia and Lymphoma Society.
- Rhubarb, along with Randy Owen of the Country Music Hall of Fame group "Alabama" and St. Jude Children's Hospital founder Danny Thomas, helped establish Country Cares for St. Jude's Kids.
- For over a decade, Jones served as Atlanta's co-host for the annual Jerry Lewis Labor Day Telethon for the Muscular Dystrophy Association.

When Rhubarb adopted me as a brother, he (like it or not) immediately became a primary planner of my family's events and vacations. Jones could weave and mesh families together and create one bigger family. I don't know how many times the Joneses, Hogans (my dear friends Jeff, Suling, and their son Taylor), and Whitlocks created a three-car train to head off for the beach, a ball game, or just to dinner. Those memories are now so very precious.

As I alluded to, Rhubarb had a big heart and it was not restricted to his public life. Countless times, I saw him display acts of human kindness. I saw the guy pick up checks for strangers at restaurants (without telling them) and buy groceries for folks who were experiencing hard times. There were no cameras or reporters around. He did it because he wanted to. He really had a big, generous heart. Whether it was in a hotel in Florida or in a restaurant in Marietta, (Jeff) Hogan and I had countless arguments with Rhubarb about who was picking up the check. He would get insulted about it at times.

Rhubarb's giving had no bounds and at times was funny. If he saw a shirt that he thought was cool, he would buy his (usually a XXXL) plus an additional XL—and he could not wait for me to come get it. Hat purchases were always in pairs. The phone would ring, and I would answer, "Scott, you won't believe what I just bought." As my stomach knotted up, I'd ask, "What?" "I just bought you a shirt with Dale Earnhardt's number three on it. I got me one and I knew you would want it." Y'all, some of the shirts and hats he bought were hideous, but he loved them, and he wanted me to have one, so I would wear them (at least once.) By the way, is anyone interested in buying a gently used XL Elvis Hawaiian shirt?

The reason Rhubarb was so willing and needing to give was likely because as a kid his family was relatively poor. Though he was born in Miami, he was reared in Tallapoosa, Georgia. Tallapoosa, in Haralson County, sits off I-20, just a whisper from the Alabama-Georgia line. He lived there most of his childhood with his mother and grandmother. From his accounts, they were a tightknit trio. Then when he found professional success, he never forgot where he came from and he loved to share what God had given him—especially with his family and friends.

Not only was Rhubarb generous, he was fun and funny. We both shared a quick wit and the ability to improvise—we could have a good time anywhere. The only audience we needed was each other. If others happened to be around that was their good luck, but Rhuby and I were usually concerned with making each other laugh—or embarrassed.

There are some great Rhubarb and Scott stories. I cannot tell them all, but here are a few examples of our escapades:

One of our favorite things to do was people watch, and to improvise their thoughts using Southern vernacular. If the passersby were talking, we would reenact that conversation. If they were just walking, we would engage in small town gossip. For example:

> *[A couple, walking by in discussion]*
> *Rhubarb: "I wish to hell you'd make up your mind*
> *and finish shopping. I want to get home to see*
> *'rasslin."*
> *Me: "You can forget watching TV, the first thing you*
> *gonna do when we get home is get the Christmas*
> *lights off the outside of trailer. Hell, it's April."*
>
> *[Well-dressed person walking alone]*
> *Rhubarb: "Look at Marylou Jennings walking*
> *around like she bought them clothes."*
> *Me: "Yeah. Everybody knows Chris Turner bought*
> *them. His car is at her house three nights a*
> *week."*
> *Rhubarb: "If Arlene finds out, they'll both be dead."*
> *Me: "Ah, Arlene knows. She just don't care. Mavis*
> *Smith at the café told me that Arlene was at the*
> *VFW last Friday with that lawyer from Shady*
> *Dale."*

We would do that and laugh our heads off. People would look at us and then try to figure out what was so funny.

* * *

Fatherhood (Grandfatherhood)

Rhubarb and Donna Jones have two daughters: Presley Frances born June 30, 2002, and Callie Reeves born in October 19, 2004. The two were the center of Rhubarb's world. He became a father very late in life, so he doted on his girls.

Another of our funny running gags went public (by accident) on the day Presley was born. We were all excited for Rhubarb and his wife Donna. I was especially happy because I knew what this meant to Rhubarb. Susan (my wife) and I scurried to the hospital to be a part of her arrival.

Now at this point, in order for the story to be funny, I must tell you since the three of us were seen so often together, there was an inside running joke among Rhubarb, Donna, and me. Due to Rhubarb and Donna's age differences, we joked that Donna and I were the couple and Rhubarb was "Grandpa." Mr. Jones was 10 years my senior and was, let us just say, a lot older than Donna. You also need to know that, as many are, Presley Jones was born a beautiful, healthy, bald little girl.

The night of Presley's birth was a celebration. Troves of people came by to congratulate the family and peek at the baby. One of Rhubarb's coworkers Jessie Jane (stage name) was among the visitors. Rhubarb was working the room—which had at least a dozen people in it. He was hugging, crying, and laughing. He was truly happy. Somehow, I had gravitated to a chair near Presley's crib. Jessie and Donna were talking and admiring the baby. As Jessie rubbed Presley's bald scalp, she turned to me while giggling and said, "Scott this baby looks like you."

Now, Rhubarb was paying *no* attention to Donna and Jessie's conversation—*until* he heard, "Scott this baby looks like you." When he heard Jessie, the look on his face as he snapped his head around was priceless. I immediately caught his look and began to scream, "No, no Rhubarb. It's not what you think.

Let me explain." The room roared with laughter and we had to explain the joke.

A couple of weeks later, when Rhubarb was holding his newborn daughter in a restaurant, a well-meaning server stopped to admire Presley. While she gushed over the baby, the server asked her, "Are you enjoying sitting with your grand-dad?" Rhubarb's face nearly blistered as it quickly reddened, Donna erupted in laughter, and I fell under the table. It was awesome!

For the record, today Presley Jones is a lovely young lady. She has a head full of hair and looks nothing like me.

Walmart

Whether on the air, in the classroom, or in a Sonny's Barbecue, for Rhubarb it was always about people. He genuinely loved performing, teaching, and being among people. That is why I think he had his Walmart fetish. Yep, Rhubarb Jones had a thing for Walmart.

Do you know why Walmart is a mega-million-dollar success? It is because they have a great business blueprint—every store in their chain is the same. The buying public knows what to expect to see when going into a Walmart. Each store stocks their selves with the same brands and they usually lay out the aisles using the same floor plan.

The above facts remove the wonder of "what's in there" for most people when they pass a Walmart. They only go to Walmart when they *need* to go to Walmart. Do you know why most people are like that? Because most people are not like Rhubarb Jones.

When he passed by a Walmart (or a Sam's Club) something in him would snap. He had to stop. I'll bet you he visited every Walmart in Georgia north of I-20 and west of I-75. While I am on the subject...

Traveling from Marietta, Georgia, to Hilton Head, South Carolina, should normally take around five hours—not when traveling with Jones. We could have three cars nose to tail headed to Hilton Head Island on I-16 doing 75 mph and we never completed the trip in less than seven. Do you want to know why? Because if that knucklehead saw a Walmart five miles ahead, he would suddenly develop a need to make a quick bathroom stop. Who goes to Walmart to pee? About 45 minutes later, we would resume our vacation and Rhubarb would have a new cap or a bag of pork rinds. We'd then drive 70 miles or so and it would happen again. While driving the next leg, he'd also call to tell me how good the pork rinds were. I am not kidding.

What should have been a five-hour trip to the beach, always turned into nearly an eight-hour, three Walmart death march. The more I would go *Ralph Kramden* on him (pretending to slowly become more and more furious) regarding his turtle-paced browsing, the more Jones enjoyed it, and the slower he walked. Macon, Dublin, Metter, Savannah, and Beaufort, South Carolina, have all experienced Scott and Rhuby on a pit stop while heading to the rental house. We never did less than two such stops, and several times, we did three. It became a rite of summer.

* * *

When Rhubarb left the Atlanta airwaves in 2008, it was bitter-sweet. For more than three decades, radio was his life, but the business of radio had changed. By that time, the people in charge had become more *corporate toadies* than *people in the radio business*. Therefore, after over three decades of excellence, the *smart guys* decided they did not need Rhuby anymore. They unceremoniously changed his station's format, bought out his contract—and poof, a Hall-of-Fame disc jockey was no longer on the air. Being blown out hurt Rhubarb but losing his daily dialogue with his fans and friends broke his heart.

My Granny taught me that the Good Lord looks after good people and he sure had his eyes on Rhuby back in 2008. Within a month of leaving radio, Rhubarb was able to fulfill a longtime dream. He became a college lecturer. He joined the faculty and staff at Kennesaw State University. While on campus, he shared his vast knowledge in the field of broadcasting with the students and he worked within our Development Offices.

For nearly a decade, he rang the bell and spread the good word about KSU and the Owls. He was all over our campaign to launch football and he bought a lot of gaudy spirit wear to prove it. I can only thank the Lord he never found a XXXL black and gold Hawaiian flowery shirt with Owl prints on it because he would have bought it (and an XL one for me—and I would have *had* to wear it).

Though he started college at LSU (that Little Southern Union), transferred to Jacksonville State, ultimately graduated from West Georgia, and 25 years later earned his master's from Shorter, Rhubarb Jones will be an Owl forever.

There is time for one more story...

Rhubarb Jones, 1960's Southern Politician

The Rhubarb Jones Golfing Experience

I loved to play golf with Rhubarb. He was an awful player. My beloved brother was a huge sports fan, a gifted musician, one of the best-read people I have ever seen, and a highly intelligent man; but he did not have one fiber of natural athletic ability. He validated that fact every time he played golf. It was really something to see. It was more than golf, it was an *experience*.

It started when he would arrive at the golf course. Rhubarb was infamous for his Hawaiian flowery shirts and the golf course was no exception. Many times he got out of his vehicle looking like a Sherwin-Williams store had just blown up on him. He would accessorize by wearing an equally loud hat and (usually) promo sunglasses. It was always something to see.

The contents of his golf bag are also worth noting. The USGA (United States Golf Association) calls for no more than 14 clubs to be in a golfer's bag. On any given day, there would be 18-20 clubs in his *orange* bag. There were always at least two putters and two drivers. Rhuby's favorite place to purchase golfing equipment was at West Georgia Golf in his beloved hometown of Tallapoosa. He was always buying drivers and putters—some of which looked nothing like a golf club.

Once we were playing golf with a young comedian named Ron White (long before his fame with the Blue Collar Comedy Tour). Rhubarb pulled from his bag the ugliest driver you could imagine. It sounded like two lead pipes clanking when he hit a ball with it. When he noticed the club and took a close look at it, Mr. White blurted out in his Texas accent, "Rhubarb, what the hell is that? It looks like a f*^#ing hubcap tied onto the end of a stick." I fell out of the cart laughing. At that moment, I knew Ron White was going to be a star.

His golf course etiquette was nonexistent. Rhubarb was loud all the time, everywhere he went, and the golf course was no exception. Serious golfers would have had nervous breakdowns playing with him. You did not even want to play in the group ahead of him or behind him. His cart and foursome were more mobile circus than golf outing. As I said, Rhubarb was loud—bigger than life everywhere all the time. If *Foghorn Leghorn* had been human, he would have been Rhubarb Jones. He talked all the time, he even talked while he was swinging. Since it did not bother him to do that, he also talked while the members of his group attempted to play. He *never* watched his ball after hitting it.

Any golf report about Jones would not be complete if I failed to comment on his actual golf skills. For me, it was pure entertainment—bad golf, but pure entertainment. I was always his de facto swing coach.

His swinging at a golf ball was never a guarantee there would be contact. I constantly had to remind him to "step up to the ball." I witnessed scores of whiffs over the years. Each were uniquely hilarious because you never knew what was going to come out of Rhuby's mouth after each whiff. If he did hit the ball, no one ever knew where it might go. *If he hit it*, he never followed this ball while it was in flight.

This best sums up Rhubarb Jones the golfer and the experience of playing with him:

One summer while vacationing together on Hilton Head Island, we decided to play an early morning round of golf. We got a time and off we went. Rhubarb was dressed as you might think—American flag cap, multicolored Hawaiian shirt, cargo shorts, and golf sandals. It was a sight. I do not remember the name of the course, but it was a fine course with wide fairways and welcoming greens. You should have seen the young woman at the counter when she turned and saw Mr. Jones. It was classic. We began our round, and as was the custom, Rhubarb was hacking away and I was laughing at him. He changed drivers twice, asked me for advice before every shot, and was in the midst of using every swear word in his vast repertoire. As usual, Rhuby was loud and never stopped talking.

To aid the golfers and the pace of play, nearly every golf course has markers on each hole 150 yards from the center of its greens. This course was no different. Some courses have their 150 plates in the ground on the fairways; some have the markers on the cart path. The course that Rhubarb and I were playing had a **three-foot high, barbershop striped pole** in the center of all 14 of its fairways—150 yards from the center of its greens. I digress.

As I said, the day's round was going as usual. Somewhere on the back nine, Rhubarb produced a 4-wood from his bag. He began to hit it off the tee. He then began hitting that 4-wood on every shot—the tee, the fairway, and rough. No matter the lie, he could only hit that 4-wood about 170 yards—no more, no less; but, to his credit, he actually was hitting the ball pretty well with that 4-wood. Mind you, he never stopped talking and *he never followed his ball's fight*, but he was hitting the ball with that 4-wood.

On about the 15th or 16th hole (a par five) Rhubarb and his 4-wood had gotten the ball about 165 yards from the green. Once we arrived at his ball, he asked me about the distance. I gave him the number and told him to use the 150-marker for his alignment; then out came the 4-wood.

In the middle of him telling me about his gained confidence in his club and hitting his third shot, a loud *BANG, BANG* rang out. Rhubarb flinched and I laughed so hard I nearly had an accident. "Where'd my ball go?" he asked, as usual. I then, with tears in my eyes, had the pleasure of telling him to look about 100 yards behind us. Folks, when he hit the ball, it immediately struck the hole's **three-foot high, barbershop striped 150-yard marker**; the ball then came flying directly back over his head—missing him by less than 12 inches and had landed 100 yards to his rears. If the ball had hit him, it would have killed him.

Upon learning of what had happened, Rhubarb put the 4-wood in his bag, got in the cart, and told me to kiss his ass. As we drove back to his ball, I asked him why I was receiving his wrath. He informed me that he could not believe I was laughing so hard. He said, "I don't know what's so funny you S.O.B. What would you have done if that ball had killed me?" To which I replied, "I'm sorry, but I wasn't laughing about the ball nearly hitting you, I was laughing about the fact that that was the first time I had ever seen you hit a ball where you were aiming." He cussed me out (again) and we finished the round.

Man, I wish we could play tomorrow.

* * *

His People

Rhubarb died suddenly on Sunday, April 2, 2017. He had a massive heart attack while sitting in the automotive section of the Walmart in Bremen, Georgia. He was having his car repaired.

While preparing his eulogy, I got to thinking about Rhubarb and his love of people—when it finally dawned on me. Rhubarb was not seemingly obsessed with *Walmart*. Every time he went into one of those stores, he was fulfilling his desire to be among and to interact with the folks that shopped there. Walmart shoppers *WERE his people*. They were both his professional and personal demographic. *He was one of them*—goodhearted, imperfect people who worked for a living and loved their family.

I have come to believe it was only appropriate that God decided to have him be among *his people* as he began his trip to heaven. He was always happiest when in the midst of his people. I praise God that he allowed me to be one of Rhubarb Jones' people.

I must confess that a little bit of me died that April day in

Bremen. Losing Rhubarb has created a void in my soul that will never fully heal. As I said earlier, for me, he was *the guy* that could make me laugh or feel better in any dark moment, as I try to make it through this world. By no means was he a perfect guy, but he was my guy. I am so glad we chatted the day before he left. He was my buddy and my brother. I miss him dearly.

Me and Rhuby

7

BILL HILL

For most of the 1980s and 1990s, Kennesaw State's golfers were coached by a salty, crabby Pennsylvanian named Bill Hill. He was not your typical golf coach. Bill was blue collar to the bone. He was a dear friend. We lost Bill Hill to colon cancer in 2000, much too early.

In the early days of our department, we utilized numerous *part-time* or *volunteer* coaches. My friend, Bill Hill was one of those people. During his tenure as coach, KSU's golf teams enjoyed success. His teams won. He would always find a way. He accomplished, on a part-time basis, more than most of us did working full time. I still admire that.

Bill was a full-time employee of Kennesaw State's Physical Plant. Notice I said *employee* and that I never accused him of working. He would not appreciate it if I had made such a dastardly accusation. We were at KSU for 15 years together, and to this day, I never knew what his real job was, but that was Hill.

Other than coaching, Bill Hill took delight in five things (in order): golf, beer, kidding his beloved Bonnie, bragging on his kids (Billy and Betsy), and sparring with his friends.

Not once in 15 years did he ever call me the morning after a softball victory, but let one of my teams lose—just one game...

The morning after a loss always started the same. I came on campus, went to my office, sat down and the phone would ring. I'd answer, "Hello." He would say, *"What the hell happened?"* And we were off. For 10 or so minutes, he'd badger while I defended. That's the way it was with Bill and me. For that matter, that's the way it was with Bill and everyone.

* * *

This is my favorite Bill Hill story:

When Bill was diagnosed with colon cancer, we were all devastated. He did the surgery, the chemo, the whole nine yards. Through it all, he kept his sense of humor. He kidded himself and the disease, just as he continued to pick at all of us. One day, near the end, we were playing together in a charity golf tournament when we met the two players with whom we were paired. He introduced us by saying, "I'm Bill Hill, I've got cancer, this is Scott Whitlock, and he stinks [at golf]." At least, I think he meant golf. You never knew with Hill.

That day, on the golf course, we laughed and entertained more than we ever had. We had the two guests hitting and poking each other, laughing the entire day. On the few occasions that he hit a poor shot and drew laughter, he'd bark "You'd laugh at a cancer patient?" I'd reply, "Only if it's you!" Silly stuff like that made up the entire day. It was the finest day I have ever had on a golf course.

While waiting between holes I'd asked him, "How ya doin' Bill?" He'd say, "I'm all right." I could tell he was tired, but when it was our turn to play, he was the first one up and at the ball. I remain truly moved by his enthusiasm that day. He was just happy to be playing. At the end of the day he said, "Thanks partner. It sure was good to be out here playing. I just wish that

I would have had a better person to play with." He laughed and so did I.

That day I witnessed a man take time away from dying to enjoy the sport and people he loved. He never complained nor whined. He just went out there and played. He played for the love of the sport. He played just to be playing. He enjoyed every minute of it and made sure that our two guests were entertained. We didn't win that golf tournament, but no team had a better day! You know, there's something to be said for *playing just to play* and sometimes your score just doesn't matter!

I miss you, Bill.

8

MARCH 21, 2013; A SAD DAY

Today, March 21, 2013, was a sad day. Our beloved yellow Labrador retriever, Luke the Dog, left us. He was 13 years old. He just crawled under our deck (a place he never went) and died. He survived three operations and lived most of his life with chronic hip problems and he died an old dog—an old lovable, sweet lump of a spoiled yellow lab.

Luke the Dog was a present to me from a former player, Blake Baskin. He was the only member of the Whitlock family with a pedigree and he knew it. Luke the Dog was the best pet I ever had. Though he was technically my dog, he became my son's and daughter's brother, he *was* my wife's baby, and I ended up being the guy that lived in HIS house.

I realize my family's story of *being so attached to our pet dog* is not unlike the stories of other families and their pets. Nearly all of us have lost a pet and have pet stories. But damn it, Luke the Dog was different. He was one of US and we were not prepared for him to go. His departure has opened up huge wounds and has created some real problems. Luke had a very specific list of duties and responsibilities around our house and now we have no one to do them. We are now a group of humans who don't know exactly what to do. For instance:

Who is going to ignore me when they see or hear the door on my side of the garage go up?

Every day, when Susan's side of the garage went up, Luke the Dog would bolt from wherever he was (inside or outside the house) to go greet *Ma-Ma* (he called Susan "Ma-Ma"—strangely enough, he sounded like Elvis when he said "Ma-Ma"). It was always such a joyful reunion. He would stand at the car door until it opened and then he'd try to jump in. *Ma-Ma* was home!

There was also a daily *non-ritual* that never occurred—it concerned MY arrival home. Each day, when my side of the garage went up, nothing happened! And, I mean **nothing**. *This always ticked me off, and I know he did it just to spite me.* I have witnessed that dog do backflips (and stick the landings) for Susan coming home from Kroger. I could come home from a 10-day road trip and there would be no Daddy's home celebration. He would just look up at me as I walked by and ask, "Where's *Ma-Ma*?" Smartass dog.

The only exception to his policy pertaining to me was when Susan traveled for more than two days. Luke the Dog would then go into his *just in case mode.* During those desperate times, when I would get home, he would just walk over to me—sans a backflip—and just stare. In a lot of ways Luke the Dog was a pragmatist. After a couple of days of no Susan, he always decided that it wouldn't hurt to suck up to me a little bit (in the unlikely case *Ma-Ma* wasn't ever coming back).

Who is going to come over and stare at me when I am worrying about a game (or just being grouchy)?

Whenever I was feeling crabby, Luke the Dog would walk over and just stare at me. By so doing, it seemed that he was sarcastically saying, "OK let's get this over with...*No matter what, I still love you daddy, that ole sun's gonna shine tomorrow, turn that frown upside down, blah, blah, blah—NOW FEED ME SOMETHING!"* That stare of his always humbled me. It reminded me that my only assets (as he saw it) were my thumbs. Having thumbs, allowed me to use a can opener—therefore, I was occasionally of some use to him. *You see, the quest for food was always the common denominator when it came to Luke the Dog.*

To whom now are we to apply human characteristics and attribute human comments?

It was a common game around our house to take turns interpreting what Luke the Dog was thinking or saying. He was quite pompous to the fact that he ran the house. *He was not our pet dog, we were his pet humans—and he knew it.* Anyway, all of us loved to tell the others what Luke just said or what Luke wanted. He would summon *Ma-Ma* (sounding like Elvis) or would *request* to be allowed to sit at the dinner table.

One of my favorite bits was that each year, after visiting my CPA John Herschel Lill III, I would tell people, "This is the last year I let Luke the Dog do my taxes." I can just see him now wearing his green visor, pencil wedged in his paw (he had no thumbs) and staring at his manual adding machine.

One of our biggest problems is deciding who's going to walk Susan every night?

Rain or shine, hot or cold, the routine was consistent. Before bedtime, usually around 10:30 p.m., Susan needed walking, and Luke would take her. It was during those walks that, I suspected, they talked out their day with Luke nightly lobbying to move upstairs. Though I have no proof, I am sure my name likely came up regularly during those walks. *I must confess I am not the easiest with which to live, so it is likely my "residential status" was discussed during many walks.* I don't know which of the two would talk the other one into letting me stay—perhaps they took turns (*I have had issues with both through the years*). Either way, I'm just grateful it always worked out for me. I like our house.

In this most recent time of reflection, I sure hope that Susan was the one doing most of the convincing. If it was the other way around—I have just lost one hell of a lobbyist—and am in big trouble.

Who is going to get us up on time?

Luke woke us up around 5:30 a.m. every—and I mean every $*%^ morning. That stinking dog had no regard for days off. He didn't even respect holidays. Now, I don't think he was an atheist, but I know for a fact he didn't respect Easter or Christmas.

Ever evolving, our 100-pound alarm clock developed his very own, unique type of snooze button. In his later years, he'd yelp once at 5:30 a.m., then again at 5:40 a.m. At 5:45 a.m., if he had not been addressed by his *Ma-Ma* and asked to come upstairs, a loud, continuous barrage of barking ensued. *At our house we never had to call the dog, the dog called us.* Now, either Susan or I will have to learn how to set the alarm clock. Damn.

Who will now have the job of flopping themselves upon the sofa and making it impossible for anyone else to sit down?

Wait...I can do that one.

Who's going snuggle up with my wife on the floor of the living room under a blanket to watch TV?

In the early days of our marriage I used to have that job, but for the last 10 years that task has nearly always been Luke the Dog's. He became very clingy to his *Ma-Ma*. They were always near one another when indoors. He had to be wherever she was. The only time he faced loneliness was when Susan would go into our bedroom—the only area of our seven-room estate from which he was banned. Even on those occasions, he never surrendered. He would walk directly up to the doorway of our bedroom (as if it were the 48th parallel) and throw himself onto the floor or against the door (if closed). He always staked out that location and was always so happy when *Ma-Ma* reappeared.

There are more things that Luke the Dog did for us daily, but in respect of brevity, I'll stop here.

It may be cliché, but Luke the Dog *was part of our family* and, like all of us, he had responsibilities. I know we will have to face all the inevitabilities and deal with the sadness that comes with our loss, but right now we have a more immediate problem. There are a lot of things that need to be handled around here daily and Luke the Dog is no longer available to serve. We don't know what to do. The Whitlocks are currently at a loss. I guess we'll figure out something and make the adjustments, but right now the future looks grim.

Luke the Dog

God has another good ole dog up there tonight in heaven—a loveable, sweet lump of a spoiled yellow lab named Luke the Dog. Lord, in case he hasn't already told you, Luke the Dog likes to be fed around 11 p.m. each night—*right after he walks Susan.* We'll miss you, buddy.

9

DR. BOBBIE BAILEY

D r. Bobbie Bailey was first introduced to the Kennesaw State softball program in the winter of 1991. KSU was in its first season of fastpitch competition when then-KSU President Dr. Betty Siegel introduced "Miss Bobbie" to KSU's young softball coach. We quickly developed a unique and genuine friendship.

Dr. Bailey, who had sponsored and managed the Atlanta-based Lorelei Ladies traveling softball team from 1960-1980, took an immediate interest our program. She quickly adopted the Owl softball program as her own. As they say, the rest is history.

Her impact on the KSU softball program was immediate—and now legendary. Initially, her support came in the form of annual scholarship donations for players. Over time, her personal interest in the program grew and her philanthropic support addressed additional needs within the program.

Since Dr. Bailey (*and the Bailey family*) joined KSU's team, over $2 million have been generously provided by the Bailey family for scholarships, facilities, and the overall enhancement of student-athletes' experiences.

Among her many gifts to the Owls was a $1 million lead gift in 2001 for the construction of what became the **Bobbie Bailey Athletic Complex**—the current home of Kennesaw State's baseball and softball programs.

In 2006, (*to honor her family*) $300,000 was again given by Miss Bobbie for the naming rights of the Kennesaw State softball stadium. Those funds enabled stadium upgrades, including a new scoreboard.

On October 4, 2008, **Bailey Park** was dedicated. Today, **Bailey Park** continues to be a special place to be an Owl softball player.

The years have seen Kennesaw State's softball program regarded among the nation's most respected. Hundreds of young women have earned degrees and dozens of championships have been won. None of those accomplishments would have been reached had it not been for the vison, kindness, and commitment of Dr. Bobbie Bailey.

In recognition of her significant impact on both the KSU Athletic Department and the Owl softball program, Dr. Bailey was inducted into the Kennesaw State University Athletic Hall of Fame in 2006. She will always be an Owl legend.

On Saturday, July 25, 2015, I took a phone call from KSU's then-President Dan Papp. His voice broke as he told me that "Miss Bobbie" was gone. She was 87. Now three years later, the complete numbness that I felt upon hearing that news has not fully gone away.

* * *

I was asked to speak at a memorial service that celebrated the life of Dr. Bailey. I consider it one of the highest honors of both my personal and professional lives. Following is that speech.

Dr. Bobbie Bailey

In the Merriam-Webster Dictionary, the phrase *role model* is simply defined as, *"someone who another person admires and tries to be like."*

I first met Dr. Bailey in the fall of 1991. KSU's-then President, Dr. Betty Siegel, arranged a meeting when, through their friendship, she learned that "Miss Bobbie" had once sponsored a traveling women's softball team—the Lorelei Ladies. Dr. Siegel immediately knew that her softball coach (me) needed to know Bobbie Bailey.

I have often said that Dr. Betty Siegel was the "mother of my career, and that "Miss Bobbie" was my career's "Fairy Godmother," because she made wishes come true.

We had just started our fastpitch program at KSU. Although our first meeting lasted only about 10 minutes, I immediately saw that her interest in our softball players and the experiences that were being offering to them were genuine; but I had no idea of the wonderful adventure on which she was about to take the Owl softball program—the scholarships, the facility, and the stadium. It was greatly due to her and the Bailey family's kindness that the softball Owls grew from a regional contender into national champions. I firmly believe that if there had not been a *Bobbie Bailey*, my coaching career would not have been the *fairy tale* that it was.

Hundreds of female athletes had their athletic experiences enhanced—or in some cases, made possible— because of her caring and commitment.

I am not trying to be overly maudlin, but her belief in the Owls and their coach provided us with that *little push, that support*, which can mean the difference in being good or being great. Without a doubt, Bobbie Bailey helped make us great.

Over the past several days, the word *opportunity* keeps coming to mind when I think about Dr. Bailey. In so many ways, her life was about *opportunity*. Early on, she worked at gaining opportunities for herself within a male-dominated business world. After beating the odds and after achieving professional success, she did not rest nor become complacent. She then committed herself to *service* by helping to provide opportunities for others.

Long before it was fashionable, she was shattering glass ceilings for women in business, in the arts, and at play. It was important to her that girls and women were afforded the same opportunities as boys and men no matter the arena.

She was fearless, and her *commitment* to that cause was infectious.

Miss Bobbie was also a teacher. She taught me to use my voice to support equal opportunity for women in collegiate sports—and believe me at times she could be a very blunt and stern instructor.

Once, in the middle of a meeting, she chewed me out for not speaking up passionately regarding a matter. She literally roared at me in a room full of people, "Scott, if you sit there with your mouth shut, they'll run all over you." The folks in the meeting really did not know what do or say while I sat there as she provided my *lesson of the day*, but everyone laughed when I responded by telling her, "Miss Bobbie, I was just waiting on YOU to stop yelling at them and I was going to pick up where you left off." She even smiled at that one. **Oh, by the way, on that day, we gained approval for the Bobbie Bailey Athletic Complex at meeting's end. After what he had just witnessed, not even Roger Hopkins dared to deny it after hearing from Dr. Bailey.**

To me, that day typified Dr. Bailey. She championed a cause, urged others to speak up for "what is right" and did not stop until the job was done. To so many here today, she was indeed a *"role model."*

Over the years, I gained part of my overall philosophy on life from the great American storyteller Theodor S. Geisel (known to the world as Dr. Seuss— *I'm sure, for those of you that know me, that fact does not surprise you).* Dr. Seuss once said, **"Don't cry because it is over. Smile because it happened."** I would like to close by stating that parts of my heart and soul will forever "smile" because Dr. Bobbie Bailey "happened" to me.

10

LEXI

Lexi Kaiser has cerebral palsy. She does not want to have it, but she cannot get rid of it. That stinks.

Lexi is a triplet. As I write, she is 16 years old. She wrestles with her condition every day. *Correction: She and her family wrestle with her condition every day. Her two triplet siblings Kelly and Trey, her younger sister Hallie, and her parents Chip and Christie assist Lexi in her 24/7/365 fight to acquire just a bit of normalcy. It is an extraordinarily hard situation.* They inspire me to try to be a better person.

I first met Lexi several years ago. Her dad Chip was our "T-shirt guy." He has screened many a practice T-shirt and hoodie for the Owls. He and I have always liked each other, but after I met Lexi, I was no longer just a customer. Without any real say so, the Kaiser's—*longtime Georgia Tech fans*—had to join the Owl Nation.

Let's stop right here. Lexi's paternal grandfather is **Roger Kaiser**. I am over a dozen sentences into this chapter and have yet to mention him. He will never forgive me for it taking this long.

Around metro-Atlanta and Dale, Indiana, Roger is a fairly well-known man. In 1961, he became Georgia Tech's first basketball All-American. After college, he went on to enjoy a storied collegiate coaching career that saw his teams win four national titles. Though I knew who he was and respected as well as admired his work, I really did not know him until Lexi arranged our meeting each other. Since fate threw us together, Coach Kaiser has become a confidant, a mentor, a fishing buddy, and a dear friend.

Coach Kaiser and his lovely wife *Miss Beverly* are regular dinner partners with the Whitlock family. Miss Beverly will even fuss at me if she thinks I need it and Roger has never once dared to attempt to save me. They are two of the most beautiful people I know. I love them dearly. They are a big part of *Team Lexi* and a big part of my story with Lexi.

Roger and Beverly Kaiser

Coach Kaiser and I love to kid each other, but there is one thing about him that drives me nuts. As I mentioned, he's earned a bit of notoriety in our area. Therefore, when we go out I can rarely enjoy a dang meal, a game, or a play without some Yellow Jacket loving yahoo coming up and asking him, "Are you ROGER KAISER?" After they leave, he will just look at me and grin. It is awful to endure.

I mentioned his name once while speaking at a coaching

clinic in Indianapolis. Upon finishing my presentation, a guy comes up and proudly tells me that his mother was Roger Kaiser's second grade teacher. I had to stand there and act like I gave a damn. I meant no disrespect to him nor his mom—I am certain that she was a lovely lady and a great teacher, but I have less than no interest in learning the names of all who educated Roger Kaiser.

Though I cannot prove it a fact, it is my strong suspicion that Roger Kaiser pays people to *recognize* him everywhere we go.

As I was saying before being sidetracked, Chip was our T-shirt guy. When he would make a delivery or me a pick up, we would always take time to visit. We'd chit chat, laugh, and enjoy small talk. It was during one such visit that Lexi was truly placed on my radar and in my life. That changed a big part of my outlook on life. I knew that Chip and Christy had triplets, I am sure that I was told of Lexi's situation, but it had never registered with me. Let me tell you, brothers and sisters, after that night *it registered*.

On this particular evening, I went by Chip's house to pick up some shirts. We began to visit, and the usual questions were being asked. Eventually, I got around to "How are the kids?" He replied, "Ah, pretty good. We are having a little trouble with Lex. She gets upset when Trey, Kelly, and Hallie (her younger sister) go out to ride their bikes and play and she can't."

BOOM.

Chip's response struck me in a way that I still cannot fully articulate. I know that I immediately felt humbled and ashamed.

After hearing the word "bikes" in Chip's answer, I immediately thought of my purple Sears Spyder bike from when I was a kid. I had not thought about that for at least 25 years.

When I was about 12, Travis, Mark, and Randy Batchelor's

folks had gotten them three new red bicycles. When I saw them, I went to my Pa-Pa and whined. A few days later, my purple Spyder bike was at my house.

I do not know if it is this way anymore, but to a country kid in 1974, having a bicycle was a big deal. It was a status symbol and it was transportation. It was independence. Standing there, my mind went back to the days of riding my bike, making Evel Knievel ramps and trying to do wheelies. I do not think I totally appreciated what my bike meant to me until Chip mentioned that his kid was upset. For some reason to me, it became unacceptable that Lexi did not have a bike.

"What do you mean?" I asked. Chip said, "You know. Trey and Kelly can go out and ride and Lexi cannot." I began to get anxious. He then went on to mention that they had been doing some research and found that bikes for kids like Lexi are made, but they are a bit expensive. Hearing that, I blurted, "How much?" He replied, "Just under $2,000." Without flinching or thinking, I said, "Order the bike!" Chip looked up at me and I said, "The KSU softball team will raise the money to pay for it. Order it!"

As I stood out in his driveway and listened to Chip speak to Lexi's frustration, I did an immediate inventory on my lot in life and was embarrassed with the findings. I realized that I was a person who enjoyed professional success. I have beautiful, healthy children. I spent my days working with talented athletes who could run, throw, jump, and do anything they wanted. Yet as I was busy enjoying my gifts, I was failing miserably in seeing the bigger picture that was directly before me. I was missing the opportunity to use my gifts to their full potential. I was missing the joy that comes when you help someone else.

That night it dawned on me that all my blessings meant nothing because I was not using them to the fullest. I realized that whereas I may not be able to help everybody, I can help one kid get one bike. I was no damn good if I chose to neglect that opportunity.

The next day I shared my experience of the previous night with our team. They were all in. A few weeks later Lexi got her bicycle at what was the first of now II *Lexi's Night* events at Kennesaw State. Seeing our players roll that bike out to her at home plate was truly a great moment to witness and a highlight of my career.

Now I must digress, while we were planning on how to get and give Lexi her bicycle, is when Chip gave me my first real introduction to Coach Roger Kaiser. As I have already stated, we bonded and became (and remain) dear friends.

Coach Kaiser assisted me in finding a source for a bike. He even got us a better deal. I also found out that Roger had started a golf tournament (*Lexi's Game*) to help the family meet the constantly straining needs Lexi faces.

Soon after our *Lexi's Night* joined *Lexi's Game* on the annual calendar, a group of family friends came together with a vision that has become a tradition. **The Alexis Kaiser Foundation** was formed. Its purpose is not only to assist Lexi, but it also allows Lexi to help other kids and families who face similar challenges. We at KSU softball jumped at the chance to participate in that endeavor.

Beginning with the second *Lexi's Night* at Kennesaw State, once a year prior to an Owls home game, Lexi comes to home plate and presents a gift to another child (usually to a stranger) and their family. Some years it is a bike, or an iPad, or another item that can enrich their life.

Sharing a moment with Lexi

To be selfish about it, during *Lexi's Night*, I feel better about myself than I do about any other day of the year. It warms my soul to see college athletes, fans, families, and friends come to our stadium to show Lexi and her special guest that they are never alone.

One of the biggest perks of the entire thing is that Lexi has decided that I am *her* coach. She even calls me "Coach." She only calls Roger Kaiser "Poppa," but she calls me "Coach." Every time she does, I just look at him and smile. As I told you, we both love to laugh.

I advise anyone who has a platform—*even if it is a tiny one like being a small college softball coach*—to not try to change the entire world. Rather, use your perch to work towards brightening the world of one person nearby. It's OK to do something, *even if it is small*, if it will have a large effect on the bigger picture. In addition, you will be richer for it.

When you get right down to it, I've gotten the better of the whole deal. All Lexi got was a bike. By opting to make a minimal effort, I ended up adding to my family of friends and I get to watch her help others the way she helped me.

In conclusion, *do not* attempt to tell me that all the above was just some set of happenstances that fell into place. I know that the Good Lord above knew that I needed to be humbled and to grow and he sent Lexi to teach me that lesson. Thanks kiddo.

11

THREE OLD MEN

How old is *old*? What qualifies something or someone as being old? Is it attitude? Is it appearance? Is it simply the number of days, months, or years something or someone has existed?

The Varsity (home of one of the world's great chili dogs) once had a slogan, "No food over 12 hours old." In the 1960s that sounded cool. They don't use it anymore. Why? In today's world, if a restaurant were to boast that fact, a group of protesters would form in about 20 minutes and gripe about the food being too old—and how it's killing our future or preventing cooks from getting jobs. Then, most of those same people would go home and eat *leftovers* because they are too lazy to cook.

I understand progress and the laws of nature. Things that are young become old. Facts are facts. What I do not understand is why a bedroom dresser becomes valuable when it is 75 years old, yet, in the eyes of many, human beings' ideas and opinions begin to devalue at age 50.

For the life of me, I cannot see why so many of today's younger people—who are supposedly more educated than ever before—fail to recognize, and take advantage of, the rich resources that are around them nearly every day—their *elders*. Why can they not see the valuable knowledge available if they would just spend time with people who have actually experienced life? To *old folks*, life is not theory. It is not ideas sold in books. To those of us that have more miles in the rear-view mirror than we do in the windshield, life is experience—*real* experience—*actual* successes and failures.

My grandparents were, at times, my primary caregivers. So, luckily for me, I have lived a life where I was eager to learn from my elders. After a half century of living, I am proud to still be somewhat dependent on and learning from my elders. My childhood circumstances spurred it, but I have always enjoyed hanging around my elders—particularly old (or older) men. Today, many young folks avoid the 60+ crowd. I never did. Perhaps it was because my dad and I were too different to ever truly connect. I don't know why, but somehow, I always knew I could benefit from hearing about the life experiences of the older generation.

I enjoyed a very rural upbringing, so maybe it is a country thing, but many of the kids I grew up with enjoyed rich, real relationships with their grandparents. I come from a small town (Bostwick, Georgia, population 372) that was, in the 1960s and '70s, populated by three and four generations of families. Many of us had grandparents we interacted with on a near daily basis. I truly believe that all our lives are richer for it.

My ongoing love and respect for my elders started with my grandfather, but I learned from all the older gentlemen (and ladies) in Bostwick. I always loved to listen to their stories. I loved to hear them talk about "what's wrong with this world" or "what they'd do if..." From an early age, I learned a great deal by just listening to them.

Over the course of my life, I've been blessed to have been strongly influenced by all my elders. However, there are *three old men* that meant the most to me—three very special old men. Each member of the trio were at least one-and-a-half generations older than me. All three had personalities that were completely different from the other two. Yet, all three remain such great role models. I want to share a little about each one.

Me at 3 years old with Pa-Pa in 1964

It Started with Pa-Pa

At the core of my affection for the *old men* in my world was my relationship with my grandfather. I was his oldest grandchild, and by my siblings' accounts, his favorite. I loved my Pa-Pa. Until the day he died, each time I would visit him he would try to slip me money. Most of my traits, good and bad, I learned or inherited from Robert C. Whitlock Sr. Until I was 25 years old, he was my *main man* and I was his. He was an advisor, a confidant, and a pal. We often would cover for each other to avoid getting in trouble with Miss Mozelle, his wife and my saintly grandmother.

My Granny was the only person of whom my Pa-Pa was terrified. She could cut off one of his rants mid-word. She could shut him up when no one else could by simply yelling out his name, "ROBERT!" She scared him to death. It was hilarious.

Though Pa-Pa had little formal education, he was one of the wisest men I ever knew. He had a great sense of moral fairness but was a terribly flawed and complicated individual. He smoked Camel cigarettes, said a blessing before every meal, at times drank to excess, and had a quick temper—but got over things just as quick. He would give any friend the shirt off his back but cuss 'em out for having to do it. As I said, he was complicated.

He possessed the ability to spot phonies from a mile away and was a tremendous judge of character. He called 'em as he saw 'em and rarely minced words. Pa-Pa was an irregular Joe, a child of the depression, and a proud veteran. He was awarded a Purple Heart during World War II and didn't mind working for a living. He didn't sneak around to drink his bourbon, he believed in God, and committed his sins in public. Pa-Pa was a lot of things, but never a hypocrite.

Robert Whitlock was one of nine kids—born to a farmer (and sometime bootlegger) and his wife. My Pa-Pa had a hard upbringing. To endure the circumstances of his boyhood, he developed a thick skin and a good sense of humor (in order to keep perspective). He retained that leathery hide and sharp wit his entire life. If you were around him, you had to develop your own thick skin and be able to take a joke.

I learned the concept of a "day's work for a day's pay" from him. He taught me that the only thing this world owes a person is a *chance*—everything else is up to them. The greatest lesson I learned (by example) from him was a broad view of family. He didn't like a lot of his kinfolk, but he loved all of them. It was weird, but somehow it made sense (at least to me).

He guarded his immediate family like a lion does his turf in the jungle. He owned the loudest roar I have ever heard, and believe me, that cat (if provoked) would bite. When you get right down to it, my Pa-Pa was a hell of a man and my first best friend. *As long as he lived, gaining his approval was the greatest compliment I could receive.*

When Pa-Pa died in an automobile accident in September of 1987, it slashed a huge hole into my very soul. I hated that feeling. In all honesty, after he was gone, though my professional career flourished, I floundered for a few years personally. I lost sight of my core values, and in many ways, I was a very lonely little boy (who mistakenly thought that he had grown up).

You can read more about my Pa-Pa in chapter 2.

* * *

Me and Grace (Ma-Ma)

Enter Pop

After a couple of years of roaming in my own personal wilderness and wrecking my personal life, the good Lord sent me Mr. Linwood (Pop) Register. He and his wife Grace (Ma-Ma) adopted me into their family and saved my life. They helped me re-center and regain perspective. I could talk for hours regarding the lady who became my second mother and the difference she continues to make in my life, but in this chapter, I will primarily speak of Pop.

Pop's wife Grace was employed in Kennesaw State's business office. One of her jobs was to handle the financial dealings of a young group of coaches—of which I was one. When she met me, she must have sensed I was needy. It was through her that I met Pop and the rest is history.

Though we had met before, it was in 1988 or '89 that Pop permanently affixed himself within my world. At first, his primary role was as a fan of KSU softball and as a critic of their young coach. He quickly became so much more. Simply put, Linwood Register Sr. was one of the finest men I have ever known. He helped me finish growing up and taught me so much. He became a travel companion, a counselor, and a father figure. Just when I needed it most, Pop helped heal my soul. He filled a void and he gave me reassurance.

When Pop met me, he had already been forced into retirement due to poor health related to his heart. Following my softball exploits helped him fill the time that made up his days. He wanted and liked to be active, but his medical condition restricted what he could do. Watching us practice (oh yes, he came to practices) and play was something he could usually do —and he loved it.

If you met Linwood Register, you quickly found out he was an avid sports fan and a great listener. He loved hot dogs, the Clemson Tigers, my children, and Ma-Ma (his wife, Grace). He also gave great, timely advice.

He was very different from my Pa-Pa. For example, Pop never threatened to kill me (which was one of my Pa-Pa's favorite *go to* reactions when I would do something wrong or irritate him—which was easy to do and occurred often). Pop was a master of *positive* reinforcement before there was such a thing. His messages and advice were always centered on love. He taught me that when all else fails, real love will withstand any test. To gain the approval of Pop was a comfort. When he nodded or bragged, I knew I had *done it* the right way.

I believe it was Pop's tough upbringing that made him so genuinely grateful for life. By the time we met, he already had a rich, full life and he was proud of it. As a young man, he worked himself out of the textile mills of North Carolina and moved to Lamar, South Carolina—a small town in Darlington County. Once settled in *LAY-MAR*, as he often called it, he got a job at the local drugstore where he met and married a good woman.

He eventually forged himself a good professional life working for Sonoco, a large company based in nearby Hartsville. His job transferred him to Marietta, Georgia, in the early 1970s. As I said, long before I met him, Linwood Register had already experienced a full life. He had a wife he adored, he had raised two sons, he was a good provider, and he had two grandkids. He also had already endured open-heart surgery (his first of three).

Pop was a prankster and a bit of a flirt. I loved to hear him tell stories of his days working with our mutual friend, Gene Neal, at Sonoco or driving Mr. Henry to the Carolina football games. I don't really know if he knew what he was getting into when he got me, but I am so thankful he found me. He was one cool dude.

Pop was the perfect *successor* to Pa-Pa within my orbit. He rode shotgun for me during the highest points of my career. He was on our team bus for as many road trips as possible. He gloated when we won (and we won often) and he consoled us all when we lost. Win or lose, he always had advice for me.

He was also crazy about my wife, Susan, and was a *real* grandfather to my children.

* * *

Maurice "Moe" Myers

Enter Moe

One of the great traditions of the NCAA Division II Softball World Series is that each participating team is assigned a host family upon arrival for the tournament. In 1999, in Salem, Virginia, Maurice and Pat Myers had volunteered and were assigned the KSU Owls. The Myers also hosted the Owls during the World Series in 2001, 2002, and 2005. Little did I know back in 1999 just how special the Myers' of Virginia would become to the Whitlocks of Georgia.

Maurice Myers, or *Moe* as he is affectionately known, is a proud veteran of the United States Army. During his years of duty, he served as a paratrooper. To see him today, you would never believe that such a gentle, quiet man was at one time such a soldier.

When I first met him, Moe was working for the city of Salem. We became fast friends. We quickly found out we were cut from the same cloth. Though he is 26 years my senior, we have many common interests. NASCAR, college football, college basketball, pro baseball, and country music are just a few of the things we both enjoy. We both also like to fish. Before we had known each other 72 hours, Moe invited me into his home to watch a car race with him and I have been welcomed in his house ever since.

In the 1999 D-II World Series our Owls posted a third-place finish. We were in town for about five days and Moe was there with us every step of the way. When we left for home I told Moe "thanks for everything" and invited him "to come and see us sometime."

* * *

Linwood "Pop" Register

Back to Pop

Pop made the trip to Salem for the 1999 series (he and Moe even met briefly), but he wasn't feeling good. Pop struggled to enjoy the trip—that should have been a signal as to the seriousness of his condition—but I guess I refused to notice it.

In the months following the '99 series I went back to my routine, Moe resumed work in Salem, and Pop's health started to decline sharply. As time passed and weeks became months, once every four to six weeks I would give Moe a call. We'd chat about whatever sport was in season, check on each other's family, and invite each other to visit. Since we were both always busy, a visit always seemed down the line.

In 2000, our team claimed national runner-up at the World Series held in Columbus, Georgia. Pop made it there for part of the tournament. He was extremely proud of us. Over the summer of 2000 Linwood Register's fragile health began to erode in chunks. Though I should have seen what was coming, I would not allow myself to believe it. For the entire time I knew him, Christmas was always important to Pop. He looked forward to it. He loved to shop, watch kids open gifts, and he enjoyed everything about the season. The 2000 season was no different except it was calmer and quieter. By late December of 2000 Pop's health was in full decline. He did not have the stamina to go shopping and *people watching* at the mall (one of his favorite hobbies) or to attend Christmas gatherings. Ma-Ma even told me in early December of 2000, "...this will be his last Christmas." Again, I refused to believe it.

By mid-January it was all over. When Pop's heart finally gave out on January 13, 2001, and God called him directly to heaven (with no waiting), I was devastated. I'll never forget the helplessness on the face of my daughter Lacey at the funeral home two nights later or my son Blake crying and his trying to figure out what had happened. I also remember that 12 years' worth of Owl softball players came home to say goodbye to the sweet old man that had brought them bubble gum and hugged them if their head coach had barked at them. Pop was buried wearing his 1995 NCAA Division II softball national championship ring.

With Pop going away that *hole* reappeared within my soul. Though I was 14 years older and finally grown, the same feeling of a lonely little boy reappeared—just like what I had felt when Pa-Pa died. I hate that feeling.

* * *

Re-enter Moe

After over a half century of living, I am convinced that the adage about *God closing doors and opening windows* is 100 percent true. As with us all, God knows me inside and out. He knows that for some reason I am a person who seeks and needs the presence (and approval) of a father figure. With my dad's personal struggles, God made certain I had Pa-Pa. When Pa-Pa died, poof—there came Pop and when he called Pop home, God sent me a Moe. I loved to please and gain the approval of all three. I guess it filled a deep-seeded need I have, but a need I didn't realize for many years.

I remember calling to tell Moe about Pop's passing. He was so sweet and listened as I rambled on about things. Looking back, it was during that phone call that Moe began to assume Pop's role in my world just as Pop had done nearly 13 years earlier after the car wreck.

While Pop was a good listener and Pa-Pa rarely listened (he was too busy *telling*), Moe is the greatest listener I have ever known. He gets the edge on Pop on the *listening ledger* because when I go off on a rant Moe will listen and rarely reply or debate. He just lets me huff and puff myself out. Pop's fatherly instincts would always push him into wanting to talk me down mid-rant. Moe just lets me get it out of my system and then we proceed. Moe never judges me. He hears everything I say to him. It works for us.

Vastly different than Pa-Pa and Pop, Moe possesses a certain style that is uniquely his. Whatever that style is (because it cannot be fully described), at this point in my life it suits me to a tee. *Everybody should have a Moe!* But you can't have mine.

Moe is someone that makes life easier. I don't have to put on airs when I am with Moe. I can even cuss! He is old enough to be my dad yet still he appreciates my company and he doesn't require much of me. He keeps everything simple. Thus, I have learned to keep things simple when I'm with Moe.

Some months after Pop's death, Moe retired from the city of Salem. This made it easier for him to come down and visit with me. Once he started his visits to Georgia (occasionally with his lovely wife Pat), they have never stopped. They are always eagerly anticipated by both of us. Three or four times each year the Whitlock house in East Cobb County becomes Moe's outpost. His visits usually last three to five days. They are never long enough, and we always try to plan the next visit while he is in town. We now even have a room in our house we refer to as "Moe's Room."

As I said, God knows what I need. He knows my limitations and he is highly aware of what I need to help me muddle through my journey. He has provided me with three distinctly different security blankets. Pa-Pa was a lion protecting and teaching his cub. Pop was a teddy bear who offered reassurance. Then there's Moe—a loyal, loveable hound dog of a man and a perfect companion.

Moe Myers now has the burden of being *my main man*. We live eight hours apart, we see each other for maybe a total of only 20 days a year, but Moe is my guy. He has nicely filled the emptiness I felt when Pop left—just as Pop had done when Pa-Pa died. Maybe it's because I am older, maybe I have grown up a bit, I don't know. At this time and place in my life, I could not have a better sidekick than Moe.

When I introduce Moe to people, I describe him as my "second dad" or my "dirty uncle." The latter description is a complete falsehood—Moe Myers is one of the sweetest, gentlest men I know. He would never knowingly offend anyone, but my calling him a "dirty uncle" embarrasses him and it makes me laugh, so I will keep doing it.

Mr. Maurice Myers is a native of Salem, Virginia. He now resides in the neighboring town of Shawsville. There is a railroad track beside his house. The trains always scare me to death the first night of any visit.

Moe is a proud graduate of Salem High School and remains a diligent, loyal follower of its football team. During football season, my weekend is not complete until Moe calls and gives me the score and his thoughts of Salem High's game from Friday night. In addition to sports, Moe loves his family, his church, working with his hands, traveling, fishing (with his buddies), and other things.

He adores his wife Pat. He is also, like my grandfather, terrified of his wife's wrath. They are so cute together. Pat knows that (like Pop) Moe can be a bit of a flirt, but she also knows he is too scared of her to ever try. She even makes fun of him and tells me about "Moe and the girls at her office" or "Moe and the pedicurist that he tips 50 percent each visit." She is always providing me tidbits about Moe the *ladies' man*. Now, before anyone gets the wrong idea, let me provide some perspective— Moe is in his 80s. Just how much trouble could he really get into?

Moe loves to come down to his outpost (my house). Other than home, he is more comfortable with me than anywhere else. We just fit. We appreciate each other. I'm the loud mouth comic and he is the stoic (sometimes slyly grinning) straight man. I accuse him of the most awful (always fabricated) things —from flirting to showing up drunk (he's a teetotaler) to taking over my house. He always denies the charges. Everyone (except Pat) always sides with him, then they condemn me—and we all laugh.

Maurice Myers is a man who is extremely grateful for the life he has. I have never seen him truly unhappy with those in his company—no matter the occasion. He views every day as a gift from God, he makes no unreasonable requests of anyone. It must feel so good to be Moe—oh, how I envy that.

Moe with several members of the 2008 KSU softball squad including (L-R): Angela Lopez, Sarah Hesterman, Amanda Malcom, and Brittany Matthews

* * *

Final Thoughts

Though Pa-Pa and Pop are watching from heaven these days, Moe is still hanging in there with me and I love him for it. In fact, I love all three of the unique characters about whom I have just written. Each had a specific role to play in my life. They taught, reassured, and supported. I owe so much to those *three old men*. I cannot imagine my life without them.

I do not know a lot, but I do know that nothing can replace life experiences in terms of learning how to navigate this world. I have learned so much from listening to and spending time with those *three old men*.

So the next time an old man (or woman) in your world offers to share a bit of their life experiences, take advantage of it. Remember, in the words of Richard Pryor— *"There ain't no such thing as an old fool, 'cause you don't get to be old by being no fool."*

Pa-Pa, Pop, and Moe were nobody's fools, but I remain foolish about them.

PART II

THINGS I'VE LEARNED

12

COACHING IS NOT FOR SISSIES

I came to Kennesaw College (now Kennesaw State University) in the summer of 1985. I was hired by a great man and a true legend in athletics within the state of Georgia, Coach James "Spec" Landrum.

In his first career, Coach Landrum was a college football coach. He has the rare distinction of coaching at both Georgia and Georgia Tech during his football days. For his second career, Coach Landrum came to Kennesaw in the early 1980s and was given the task of starting an athletic program. He did just that. By the mid-1980s, Kennesaw College, utilizing a staff made up mostly of part-time personnel, had its new athletic department up and running.

The impressive legacy that KSU's athletic department has carved has been done by building off the foundation laid by Coach Landrum.

During his tenure as athletic director (1981–87), Coach Landrum started eight varsity sports between 1984 and 1986 and hired the school's first crop of full-time coaches—including yours truly. He was both a father figure and a huge fan of a young Scott Whitlock.

I was originally hired by Coach Landrum as assistant women's basketball coach and assistant slowpitch softball coach (in the mid-1980s, fastpitch was a game played mainly by Yankees—people from north of Dalton and Californians). Basketball was my primary assignment. The head softball coach was a part-time employee of our school (she had a very good full-time teaching job); so I was assigned to handle all administrative matters for softball and assist on the field.

For the record, Coach Medra Ashmore, the head slowpitch softball coach, was a fine coach and her teams won. However, our working relationship was doomed from the start. I mean, Coach Landrum wanted me to serve as the person who "handles the money" and the scheduling. In fact, at Landrum's direction, the only things that Coach Ashmore was to be in charge of were practices and game day. How could that possibly work? Well, somehow it did—but for only one season.

From the beginning I realized there was no logical way the arrangement would work over a long run. I was 23, one of the new guys, poor and starving, so I did as I was told and did not ask any questions.

The situation was tough. Coach Ashmore was uncomfortable with having me assigned to her staff. The players, with whom she was (for the most part) very popular, sensed the tension from day one, which didn't help things. During the majority of our one-year *arrangement*, I was looked at and treated as a visitor or an outsider.

Through it all, Coach Ashmore and I worked as well as we could together. And to the credit of everyone involved with the softball team during 1986, we had a fantastic season. We won both the Georgia Conference and NAIA District 25 Championships—in those days that's as far as a slowpitch team could go.

During the summer of 1986, Coach Ashmore went to the administration to air her concerns regarding the awkwardness of our situation. What I and most of the players were not aware of at the time was that there were some issues between her and the administration at the end of the previous season (1985)—so there were preexisting circumstances neither the players nor I knew about. Anyway...

She was ultimately released from her duties as head softball coach. Then all hell broke loose. The players went nuts, parents filed complaints with the president, and no one was happy.

And guess who was immediately named to replace the successful and popular head coach who was just relieved of her duties? You got it: J. Scott Whitlock.

Even before I had my first team meeting, several of the players let it be known that my skinny butt was not wanted. They thought I had stolen the job away from their coach and began to verbally attack both Coach Landrum and me. Today, I have a qualified respect that they had loyalty toward their coach, but at the time, it was tough to take. I later found out some of the ill being sent my way was stirred by some faculty members who had a grudge with Coach Landrum. The softball players were their convenient pawns and I was simply a convenient nail on which to hang their gripes with my boss.

Later, some of the faculty advisors apologized to me for their "mistaking my involvement," and, as I always do, I took the high road (I called one an old bald bastard and threatened to kick another's butt—she's lucky I found out she was 64 and had a bad hip).

The ordeal even made the local papers and during an interview several players questioned my ability to coach. I guess they were uncertain as to my ability to coach a sport as complicated as slowpitch softball.

I did get one endorsement. When asked about the likelihood of me succeeding, the team student trainer was quoted in the paper as saying, "Oh he'll win. The players here are so good that even *Felix the Cat* could coach this team."

On a serious note, the experience of being dragged through the mud for things in which I had no part was quite frightening and unsettling for a 23-year-old college coach in only his 11th month on the job.

I had always been popular with my friends, teammates, classmates, coworkers, and players. To be criticized publicly was quite a jolt. It scared me and began to eat at me. I guess Coach Landrum noticed I was having trouble with the situation, so he played his ace in the hole. He sent me a visitor, and she came with some great advice.

Late one Friday afternoon, about five days into the ordeal, Coach Landrum's wife, Dr. Mildred Landrum, stormed into my office.

Dr. Landrum was a college professor by profession. In reality, she was Coach Landrum's secret weapon—blessed with great expertise in telling people the plain truth. She never quibbles nor stutters. She says what needs to be said—like it or not. To this day, I still lean on her frank opinions regarding various matters and I have much respect for her and love her dearly.

Once in the office, she barked to me, "Scott, Spec and I have been in this athletic business for a lot of years, so you listen to me! If you are going to make it, you are going to have to have tougher skin. If you are going to buckle every time you are criticized, you need to quit now. *Coaching is not for sissies.*"

I immediately stopped being bothered by the ordeal. I was too busy dealing with my new fear—Dr. Mildred Landrum. I am here to tell you that in about 10 seconds she took me to the woodshed, spanked my pitiful ego, and sent me back out into the world more educated.

Actually, her advice did get through to me. She reminded me that coaching is a profession that lends itself to critics and second guessers. I had to grow and work at it, but from that day on, I have never let the words and deeds of the misinformed or the critics cloud my judgment.

After a few weeks, the fuss died down and I began my first season as a collegiate head softball coach. Several of the players who had expressed reservations about playing for me were still with the team. They still somewhat viewed me as the substitute teacher and (if truth be told) I was still a bit hurt about what they had put me through.

I realized we needed to work together if the team had any chance to survive, so I requested a meeting with the returnees to *air things out*. I had no idea what would come of it, but it turned out to be one of the best moves I ever made.

In the beginning, I listened. Each one told me their thoughts, feelings, and expectations. When they finished, and some of it was tough for me to take, I made one simple request. "We can't change what has happened, so let's start over. I'm willing to clean the slate and start fresh if you are. Let's give each other a chance." It was simple as that.

To their credit, they did. We got to know each other; and whereas I never tried to replace Coach Ashmore in their hearts, they did allow me to show them I was going to be a hard-working and fair coach.

The 1987 softball team at Kennesaw State repeated the successes of the '86 team. We won a lot and lost only a few. We claimed the region and district championships. The players on that club were as good at their game as any of our fastpitch teams have been at theirs. Those gals could really play.

That first season as a head coach, I learned:

- Thick skin is a good thing to have.
- Female athletes possess great passion.
- It is important to simply be given a chance.

If the returnees of that team had not given me a chance, who knows what direction my career would have taken.

You know, looking back, the student trainer was right. *Felix the Cat* could have coached that team—they were that good. And Dr. Landrum provided me with the soundest advice I ever received, "Coaching is not for sissies."

Yep, that's me on game day - cool and calm

It's OK that most people have a misconception of coaches and coaching. The masses think we spend all our careers getting paid for having fun and playing games. We cannot, and will not, ever fully make them understand. Whereas our profession is enjoyable and fulfilling, it can also be difficult and gut wrenching.

Coaches go through a lot of ups and downs. Our lives and lifestyles are unique. It takes different (some would say crazy) types of people to let their professional successes and livelihoods be largely dependent upon the actions and inactions of young people the ages of anywhere from 14 to 23.

Remember, when you decide to be a coach, you sign a figurative waiver pertaining to public scrutiny. You invite criticism to be a present in your world—daily. You agree to be blamed. You opt to be the scapegoat.

Over my 30+ years in this business, I have learned so much; but some of my greatest lessons were taught to me during my first weeks as a collegiate head coach. At the time, the lessons were bitter medicine, but over the years, I have leaned upon them often.

Here's the bottom line: If you are going to enter the profession, stay in the profession, and want to have a shot at succeeding in the profession, here is lesson number one. Every day wear your big boy or big girl pants to work—*Coaching is not for sissies.*

13

WE HAVE A MESS ON OUR HANDS

W*arning: I did not want to write this chapter, but I could not help myself. I have to get this out of my system, so here we go...*

For the last two decades adults—due to greed, arrogance, ignorance, selfishness, and exploitation have been seemingly hell-bent and bound in ruining youth sports in America.

* * *

Life in Bostwick, Georgia, was fairly straightforward and uncomplicated. For instance, during the spring, little boys played baseball. In the fall, our game was football, and, in the winter, it was basketball. Our parents did not ask us to pick a sport on which to *concentrate* by the time we were 10 years old. We were actually allowed to have childhoods. The majority of our competitions, from ages 6 to 12, were held in someone's backyard—with no adults. And get this: there were no adult umpires or referees. We (kids) decided if a player was safe or out. We even called our own fouls in basketball and penalties in football (granted, blood usually had to easily be seen in order to get the call—but we managed).

As I sit on the porch here at the *retired coaches home* and look at today's landscape for kids playing sports, the terrain has vastly changed from what I described in the paragraph prior. I realize that we are 45 years down the road, times change, and *progress will not be denied.* In this case the change is not for the better. Youth sports have evolved, but not for the better. They were better for a while, but it has now gotten out of hand and is not what it should be.

I want to discuss what I see currently happening and what our adults are doing to our children as they play "organized" youth sports. This topic is uncomfortable and I have mixed feelings even as I write. The subject is difficult and can been seen (and argued) from several different perspectives, but I feel strongly that we need to examine the issue.

* * *

However beautiful the strategy, you should occasionally look at the results.
  Often attributed to Sir Winston Churchill

This quotation regularly races through my mind as I look at what is happening to today's children in their struggles to find fun while participating in youth sports in the 21st century—an enterprise coordinated and administered by *adults.*

* * *

1967 Bostwick Pee Wee baseball team

In the mid-1960s, as a kid during the ages of 5 and 6, I could not wait for the *moment*—the day I would be old enough to play organized ball and, more importantly, get the chance to put on my first real uniform. To me, being in uniform was (and still is) magical. A uniform was and always should be special to a player. It represents being a part of something bigger than yourself. When I was a kid, it often had the name of your *school* or *town* on it. When you are in uniform, you are a member of a select group chosen to represent everyone who cannot. It's awesome.

Back then (1967), wearing a uniform required that you be willing to protect and fight for your teammates—literally and figuratively. It was also a reminder that you were dependent on others for success. The uniform was the weld that held the parts of the group together and created the team.

I can still remember my first uniform when I played Pee Wee baseball in 1967. It was white with red piping. My second season, the word "Bostwick" was emblazoned across the front, and the number 1 on the back. I was assigned number 1 not because of my skill or position of leadership, but because I was so skinny, it was the only number that you could clearly see on my back. The uniform was polyester, heavy, and hot, but it was my uniform!

Back in the day, it was so cool to play for your hometown's team. Each of us dozen or so boys riding on the back of J.B. Ruark's or John Nunn's truck and heading to Madison, Rutledge, or Social Circle to play knew that we carried the bragging rights of our entire little town with us, and we welcomed the responsibility. It was us against whoever the schedule brought. It was competition and civic pride wrapped up into one beautiful package. It was what I believe sports were intended to be: exciting and fun.

I'll never forget my first baseball uniform. I was 6.

* * *

Looking back, there was one important thing missing back then. There were few to no opportunities for girls to play youth sports, either unorganized or structured. Societal evolution has somewhat addressed this problem. Today, there are more opportunities for young females to play organized sports and that is a great thing, but there are still gaps that need to be closed. We are not there yet, but we're gaining on it.

* * *

For kids 12 and older, today's games are vastly different. There are (in all too many cases) no longer any serious thoughts of civic or team pride or even of *winning* for that matter. The end game for much of today's youth sports is *exposure*. Look at ME, look at ME, look at MY FATHER'S CHILD.

The games and their outcomes have become *asides* to the

opportunity for players to show off their individual skill sets to impress some scout or college coach—or to stroke dad's ego or to justify all the money he has spent on hitting lessons.

The concept of *fun* in many cases is smothered by the pressure to perform. The name on the front of the jersey has become nearly irrelevant and the number on the back is only there to make it easier for the scout/coach to identify the prospect. How sad is that?

Where did the fun go?

From the beginning, the fun of sports was there for me. In addition, it was there for the vast majority of the guys I grew up with. I was never the best player or the worst (until I got older), but I had fun every day I played. Sadly, many of today's youngsters cannot make that claim.

When I write of the lack of fun in today's youth sports, I am not talking about a bad day at the ballpark or a hitting slump—that comes and goes in all sports. I am talking about youngsters who are not being allowed to simply enjoy playing. One kid not enjoying a sport, a kid's game, is one too many, and we now have thousands who do not. Why? What's to blame? Whereas I do not have all the answers, I can positively point out the primary cause. *Adults!*

Yep, you got it. The people who are classified (in many cases inaccurately) as *mature adults* are ruining youth sports. Adults are inserting their presence and desires into youth sports to such a degree that the kids have no chance in hell of having fun. The pressures placed upon the shoulders of many of today's kids, by their parents and coaches (the *adults*), leave very little space within a child's psyche for *fun* to materialize. With every move they make being critiqued and with everything they do being so closely watched by those in charge of their *well-being*, it is nearly impossible for kids to simply enjoy themselves.

Why is this happening?

There are countless elements that pollute the waters of today's youth sports. Here are some common examples:

- The good intentions of well-meaning parents that go sideways
- Greed
- Egotistical adults
- The three above reasons notwithstanding, the very core of what is wrecking youth sports is the common thread of MONEY. It's about the MONEY!

Many adults now see youth sports an opportunity to make financial investments by means of their kids; while some adults are trying to find ways to make money while *helping* the kids by fleecing ignorant and unsuspecting parents and kids. Unfortunately, some poor excuses for humans are involving themselves in youth sports strictly in efforts to stroke their own egos.

As I write these thoughts—in my 57th year (2019) and after 28 years as a collegiate head coach—my position is that grown-ups are hijacking a huge slice of our kids' lives. The *adults* have become obsessed with their kids' athletic experiences, living life through their children, or making or saving a dollar. They now refuse to let the kids enjoy this one area of their lives. Adults (coaches and *parents*) are ruining what should be a special time in their children's lives. And, none of them seem to care. Oh, they may shrug and give the circumstances lip service, but few to none seem to have the guts to scream, "ENOUGH!"

* * *

My cynicism regarding adults and youth sports started long before I began my coaching career, but it was only after three decades in the profession that my concerns were validated.

My first taste of what adults might do came when I was very young. After each of my Little League games, I would have to listen to my dad debrief me on what went wrong— even if we won. Now, when you are a 6 or 8 year old, you do not know any different, so you endure it. You just assume that it's a part of life you have to endure. You assume it's normal for some adult to yap for an hour about a Pee Wee baseball game. You just knew you had to listen and *learn* as some *wanna be* pro told you how you should have "positioned yourself differently in order to better relay the ball from left field to home plate back in the third inning." Hell, I just wanted to go to Dairy Queen.

* * *

Today, 45+ years later, I realize that my dad wasn't being a *complete* jerk. He was just ahead of his time. I now see he was actually a parent of the 21st century even way back then. He always fancied himself as quite the trendsetter. However, I digress.

After his overview, his attention would then turn to the coaches—another 20 minutes as he went on about how we nearly let the team sponsored by Madison's VFW beat us. (Madison was the biggest town in my home county back in 1968. They had three teams, so their teams had sponsors/nicknames.) It would have killed my daddy if he knew my biggest concern in life at that time was hoping he'd shut up and get me home in time to watch *Batman*.

In fairness, I was never completely stripped of my self-worth as a player or person by my father. My dad actually did know a great deal about hitting. He just could not wrap his head around the fact that someone who had only one digit in their age struggled to grasp all of Ted Williams' theories on hitting. In addition, it drove him especially crazy that the player in question really didn't care about *Teddy Ballgame's* thoughts. I just wanted to play.

I had a great athletic experience as a kid. My dad wanted me to be a good player, but he never really punished me if I was not playing well (except for the endless lectures on the sport in season). I am grateful I was allowed to be a seasonal athlete. As I said earlier, it was baseball in spring and into summer, fall meant football, and winter basketball. If I had been forced to play only one sport while growing up, I would have missed so much.

* * *

Flash forward 45+ years and back to the subject at hand. In 2018, most kids still have parents, but the parents have changed! It is a vastly different athletic landscape that many of today's children are being asked to navigate as opposed to the terrain of the late '60s. Over the past five decades, children's sports have been systematically polluted, exploited, and spoiled by those who should know better. Most of today's *sports parents* should be ashamed of themselves.

Before we go any further, let me say the problems of which I am about to speak were not created intentionally. Most adults continue to want only the very best for their young players, but they have lost the bigger picture and do not know how to just let the kids have fun playing. Somehow, the whole thing has started snowballing straight to hell.

Though it may not contain anything new, here's my take on a chunk of youth sports in America:

Adults, their egos and their money, are ruining youth sports. They're ruining it! The evolution of society that led to increased opportunities for our boys and girls is a great thing. I truly believe that most people involved wanted it to be about all that it is supposed to be. At some point, the financial snowball started rolling at a faster rate than common sense and good judgment could keep up with.

* * *

I have made quite a bit of money working in sports. My time coaching, running or working camps, and speaking at clinics has afforded me a great life. I want to acknowledge that point up front and confess that I am perhaps one of the guilty. So please know that I am not writing this from some lofty, self-righteous perch. I am writing with a bit of a guilty conscience and in hopes of spurring other people (adults) to do a bit of self-evaluation when it comes to today's and tomorrow's youth sports. I also want to encourage our current generation of parents, coaches (youth, high school, and collegiate), and instructors to be *better*. Our kids need them to commit themselves to righting the ship.

It is also worth noting that for the remainder of this chapter, I will speak from the perspective of one who has spent the vast majority of his life stumbling about while being involved in the bat and ball sports of baseball and softball. However, the essence of what I am trying to say can likely be found today in just about any *organized* youth sport in America. I urge you to insert your sport into my thoughts. At the end, hopefully, you'll likely get the message.

It started about 35 years ago with well-meaning parents.

As the Earth's population increased during the 20th century, backyards and neighborhood sandlots became fewer and fewer. Well-meaning people, seeing a need, started building parks in which their kids could play. Who were the people that funded the construction of parks? Adults. So right there, we have **Financial Investment.**

With the creation of parks, came logistical concerns— things like, "Who is going to do the scheduling and who will keep things organized, etc.?" Who was chosen to do it? Right you are—adults. Now, there is **Time Investment** (and as they say, "time is money").

As they were building and organizing the parks, some adults accidentally got the impression that they knew a little bit about a given sport. Even worse, some adults— *through no real fault of their own*—became so delusional they grew to believe they could even teach or coach a sport that they never played.

Let's pause for a moment. For many, the *coaching delusion* was not the first miscalculation of the afflicted masses alluded to in the prior paragraph. Their first error was in believing they were mature enough and sufficiently emotionally equipped to be a parent. If my 10th-grade science teacher was right, and I have no reason to doubt Mrs. Jones, there is no correlation between one's physical ability to reproduce and one's being appropriately equipped to properly rear a child. After a half century of observing, I believe everyone should have to take (and pass) a test, administered by the Almighty himself, prior to reproducing.

Hitting the Fan

After the parks were completed, the organization in place, and coaches identified was when the s*^% and the fan blades met. You know why? Right again, adults.

Parks need upkeep, and adults have egos, and both demand care and fertilization. Thus they (the grown-ups) had to address the parks' upkeep—more **Financial** and **Time Investments**.

Once there was money allotted for upkeep, the adults

figured, "Well if we are going to pay for the place, we'd better damn well be using it—all day, every day—all year round."

Have you noticed the kids have yet to be mentioned in my theory? The adults then had to go into marketing mode (**Time Investment**) and to help pay the bills, they had to encourage the use of the park. Thus, leagues had to be formed—*spring, summer, fall, and winter leagues.*

Moms and dads, at every supermarket, soon started to see flyers for league enrollment, and kids from ages 4 to 18 were urged to sign up. The first hint of the **Expense vs. Income Factor** appeared at the park.

Then it was time for game day. **Time Investment.**

Park Politics

- The first gripe: *"My kid is not playing enough."* (**Egos show up.**) Now, we were really off to the races.
- The first gripe eventually led to the first team split.
- Team splits led to a stretch in park usage demands.
- "We need a better practice time than the one we have." Eventually led to a demand for more parks.
- Then, the cycle started anew somewhere else.

What I just described were the *park politics* that existed for a long time—and much of it still exists. As ugly as that sounds, today's youth athletics has morphed into an even uglier spectacle. Get ready folks, here comes travel ball.

It is Now a Mess

Today's perils within youth athletics make park politics seem like a grand old tradition. Things like travel teams, recruiting services, showcase tournaments, skill instructors, and college coaches (offering elite, exposure camps) exist—all in the name of opportunity; however, all requiring the kids and their parents to pay up—our next sets of **Financial** and **Time Investments.**

The aforementioned land mines were perhaps created with good intentions, but they have mutated into big and dark back alleys where young athletes are treated as commodities rather than children. These pieces of the problems with today's youth sports are clouded, gray, and camouflaged. Each of the shrouded areas are comprised of an olio of personalities. Some are great people, who do things largely for the right reasons. Some are snake oil salesmen and con artists. Some are just hypocritical, money-grubbing skunks. Without dwelling too much, I would like to share some thoughts on each area.

Travel Teams

At first, the concept was a great idea. Park teams were made up of kids with wide gaps in skill and in actual interest. Many times, you could have high-level players throwing to kids who could not properly wear a glove, let alone catch a ball. The types of frustration created by such occurrences led to unhealthy situations for everyone involved. It is only natural that players of higher skills would want to play with and against kids with similar talent. That desire led to what has become known as travel teams. This would have worked out fine had it not caused more **Financial** and **Time Investments**.

The *travel* part of *travel team* should have been a clue this concept was going to run into a bit of money—and it has. Like slow, steady flowing lava, all the pitfalls that came with park politics, found their way into travel ball. But the costs (financial and emotional) multiplied tenfold.

Here is what messed up travel ball. The adults did not stay at the parks—they traveled, too. The parents of the higher-skilled players and *rich kids* left the parks and went with their kids to travel ball. So, it was bound to happen. Whereas the original travel players were usually those who had indeed developed a higher set of playing skills, unfortunately their parents were still rather lacking in their abilities to *parent*.

Just as at the parks,

- A "my kid is not playing enough" argument occurred. Every coach must be mindful that the primary desire of each parent is to make certain the team's best eight players, plus their kid, is in the starting lineup.
- Somewhere during the playing time argument, the comment, "My wife and I are paying all this money to play, we are forced to practice twice a week, then we travel on the weekends and we are not getting enough exposure for the money we spend" was made (we've now hit the trifecta—**Time, Money,** and **Ego**).
- Next came a *travel team split* and so the virus spread.

Sounds familiar, doesn't it? The problems that come with travel ball do resemble the same arguments at most parks; however, the stakes are much higher. With travel ball come the "E" words—**Exposure** and **Expense**. Once an adult becomes a travel ball parent, he or she usually enters the business of *marketing* and reclassify their child from human being to commodity. In addition, as we all know, adults are not happy when an investment of their time and money doesn't pan out.

Travel Team Coaches/Owners

I've enjoyed great relationships with travel ball coaches. Some are fine, honorable people who I consider personal friends. Most are good folks, however, today they've taken coaching youth softball and turned it into entrepreneurial endeavors. Some club teams are making so much money running "nonprofit" travel ball organizations that they no longer have *day jobs*. And they say, "It's all about the kids." Give me a break!

Families are being asked to pay tons of money for the honor of being a part of one of seven teams within travel organization X, plus they are then *highly encouraged*, by travel organization X, to pay additional cash for weekly hitting and/or pitching lessons (as provided by the organization's staff). And sadly, the families do it. They fork out thousands of dollars a year. **Money, Money, Money.**

* * *

As crazy as this sounds, I know of at least four cases in the last five years, where parents of children have borrowed money (from banks) in order to underwrite the marketing of their little darlings (making it possible for their kid to play on certain travel ball teams). Are you kidding me? Are these people nuts or what?

Families are *flying* two and three-time zones (regularly) to play for the team that "promises them the most." What the hell?

* * *

You know, I would respect the coaches/directors of the super softball organizations a lot more if they would just say, "Folks, here at team X, we are in the softball business. We will try to help your kid, but you will have to pay us for our attention and loyalty. We can make you no guarantees, but look on the bright side, we have a reasonable payment plan and we do accept both debit and credit cards."

At least if they would say that aloud (instead of their usual guff, "it's all about the kids"), it would be honest—and all could respect it.

Professional Skills Instruction

This area is a tough one for me. I am a believer in the idea that kids need to be properly taught the skills of a given sport and trained to employ the proper fundamentals. Today, thousands of parents spend millions of dollars annually to enlist the services of athletic professionals whose end game is to make a living off children and the sports they play. Parents are paying through the nose to ensure that their kid becomes the next big thing. **Money.**

Week after week, year after year, starting as early as age 6 or 8, young folks are being loaded into cars or vans, then shuttled to see *Coach Magic*, because someone told a parent at church that *Coach Magic* has been great for their prodigy. I am all for word of mouth endorsements, however, you need to weigh all the factors before turning your kid over to a skill instructor. Questions to consider:

- Are the prospective instructors actually qualified?
- Does your child really have a passion (some natural ability) for the sport?
- Can your household realistically afford the costs that come with professional instruction?
- Does your kid truly want lessons?

These are good places to start when considering going down the path of special instruction.

My brother, Don McKinlay, owns and operates a much-respected business that provides skill instruction for young aspiring softball players. He is qualified, creditable, affordable, and he does it for the right reasons. Unfortunately, not everybody is like my little brother.

Most instructors are *always* going to see the potential in your child, and they will be quite confident with another six months of lessons that, you too, will start to see the improvement. **Money.** *Remember: The end games are not the same—you are trying to make a player; the instructors are trying to make a living while trying to make your kid better.*

Now, I am not implying that all instructors are less than forthcoming regarding the *upside* of their students, I'm just saying, if you are going to seek skill instruction for a child from a *professional*, make certain they are qualified and reputable.

* * *

Look daddy, just because you spent three hours a week sitting on a bucket (for eight years), catching for your kid, while you paid someone to give him or her pitching lessons does *not* make you a qualified pitching instructor. So quit trying to recoup some of your money.

And, oh by the way mom and dad, it really didn't help a whole lot when you changed instructors five times over those eight years did it? Baby still didn't get to pitch at Alabama, did she?

* * *

Recruiting Services

I have no real axe to grind with the recruiting services. I am all for capitalism. I totally respect anyone's right to earn an honest living—and folks have a right to spend the money they earn in any manner of their choosing. I do, however, have concerns when parents outsource the responsibilities that should be theirs. Finding the right college/university for your child is important and every child's parent/guardian should be in the lead throughout that search.

The idea that a stranger can do a better job of assessing a child's educational needs than his/her parents is just foreign to me. With all the information available at our fingertips today, a parent's need to pay someone to *find the right school* for their kid is an example of laziness or apathy on their part.

Let me be clear, this is not an indictment of recruiting services. I can attest to times when a service directly led to a match between prospect and college. Any endeavor that helps a kid ultimately get to college has merit. Whereas I respect and appreciate what the recruiting services might do for kids, I am truly amazed at how many parents are willing to pay to avoid the hassles of helping their child select a school or to add one more expense to their *quest for excess.*

Showcase Tournaments

There are some people who still do things for the right reasons. However, make no mistake, the majority of these tournaments are about money. They are camouflaged by promises of competition and college coaches or pro scouts being present for an "opportunity for you (and your kid) to be seen." At the end of the day, it's really about *get their money, run 'em in, run 'em out, and head to the bank*—then go home and convince yourself that it was *all about the kids.*

Two hundred teams playing in five, 60-minute games at three different complexes—*over three days*—are not unusual schedules for showcases. Let's be honest. How can these conditions really make softball fun for anyone, and how can you expect a player to be able to receive a thorough evaluation in that setting?

In fairness, when elaborating on this topic, I must circle back to travel teams and us collegiate coaches. It's an abstract case of the chicken or the egg. If the travel teams would not go play in these cattle calls, the collegiate coaches would not patronize them. If the college coaches would not show up for such events, the travel teams would be less likely to attend. If just one of these two groups would just say "No, this is not right. We're not coming," then these types of happenings would die on the vine. Unfortunately, I am not optimistic about that occurring.

Most travel team coaches think they must go to such events, or they risk losing good players to teams that are willing to go (the parents strike again). College coaches are always going to go because they are scared that someone else will find a stud or steal an already committed **eighth-grader** (*don't get me started on that one*).

Oh well, as long as I am here...any parent who thinks their eighth-grader is refined and mature enough to commit to a given college is nuts. They are 13 or 14 for goodness sakes. You should be ashamed of yourselves. And to my peers who are now willing to ask an eighth-grader to deal with the pressures of making such an important life decision—shame on you, too. Now there, I've said it.

Collegiate Camps

As I confessed earlier, over my years associated with softball, I have made a lot of money either running or working at kids' camps. I also want to say that there are many types of camps offered by collegiate coaches, at different times each year, that are authentic *teaching camps*. Regrettably, however, many are not. To get value for money spent, parents really need to research what a kid can expect when they choose to attend a given camp. Some camps actually teach, many are just babysitting services that give you a T-shirt.

Summer overnight camps (running from Sunday night until Thursday morning—so the kids can get to a *weekend showcase*) and holiday/winter camps are the basic choices provided by collegiate camps. At the better camps, the camper-to-instructor ratio will average about 14 to 1. There are some collegiate camps that see their ratios exceed 30 to 1. (Those camps are about **Money.**)

It would be hypocritical of me to take a parent, travel team leadership, or tournament organizers, etc., to task without pointing out what is occurring in my own area within the industry (college coaching).

Thousands of kids want to play at *Big School U*, but only a few can. Yet, year after year, some of my peers advertise camp opportunities to the masses with the unspoken carrot being —*You never know, we just might pick you.* Regardless of actual skill level, thousands of kids are accepted to attend camps offered by college coaches. On occasions, a campus will host 300 kids for two days of an *elite* camp. At these camps, very little teaching takes place. The numbers simply will not allow for it. The numbers (people and **Money**) have swollen to the point that real teaching camps are a rare thing.

Now I am not suggesting that my colleagues should get out of the camp business, but perhaps it's time that they employ a little bit more truth in advertising. I propose that they simply tell the 300 attendees, "Hey, 298 of you have no chance to ever play here, the other two might. However, during this camp we will try to teach you a little bit and we'll make it as safe and fun as possible. We promise nothing more."

Conclusion

In case you missed it, the whole system has become more about the **Money, Time**, and **Egos** of adults (parents and coaches/instructors of all kinds) than it is about sports for children. We have strayed too far for too long from the core of what youth sports were meant to be.

I participated in, and prospered during, the creation of this detour of our good senses. I wish that I would have possessed better foresight. If I had, maybe I could have helped prevent it from occurring—but I strongly doubt it.

Now here I sit, five years removed from it all, looking back and seeing where we are today. It concerns me deeply. I do not know exactly how, but I do know that **SOMEBODY HAS GOT TO FIX THIS MESS.** My copy editor and dear friend, *Slim* Brown, told me that I must offer some possibilities of ways we can straighten things out, or I will be just another old man griping about "today" while longing for yesteryear.

I am hesitant to make any suggestions because I am unsure that I am qualified, and I do not know if any of my ideas will work. But I will defer to the advice of the professional writer. So *Slim*, here goes nothing...

My Immediate Suggestions

- **Parents** – Allow your kids to play multiple sports for as long as they wish. *Do not make them pick "their sport" by age 3.*
- **Parents** – Do a math exercise. Add up all the money your family will spend over your kid's childhood on lessons, travel ball, camps, recruiting services, etcetera. Then see just how close you might be to being able to pay for a good college education for your kid. Remember, in collegiate softball, a 33 percent scholarship is a good offer, and a 75 percent offer is a great one.
- **Parents** – Be realistic and use common sense. If the deal sounds too good to be true, then quite likely it is a lie.
- **Coaches** (at all levels) – Tell the truth.
- **Instructors** – Provide honest assessments to your paying customers. If you cannot help them, don't take their money.
- **All Adults** – Quit using children to make a living, to relive your childhood, or to achieve things you could not. Let them have their lives.
- **All Adults** – Let the kids have fun!
- **Players** – Please accept our (the adults') apologies. We have screwed it up.

I don't know if any of my ideas will help, and I know there are smarter people than me that see the same things I am seeing. I beg you to SPEAK UP! If you do not raise a voice, if you continue to let what's going on occur, eventually the kids will figure out that it is we (the adults) who are screwing up a big part of their childhoods, and then they will simply refuse to play anymore.

Kids will soon be spending all their free time staying indoors and playing video games instead—because they (unlike sports) are still fun. *Oh wait...that's already happening.*

14

"MISTER, YOU ARE 100 PERCENT RIGHT."

A LOOK BACK AT MY COACHING PHILOSOPHY

Many people misunderstood my coaching style, or they found it antiquated. You see, I was an *old-school* coach. I was vocal and demonstrative at practices and on game day. It was not uncommon for me to issue emphatic challenges to my players—any time or anywhere. If you are a stranger to me or our program, when you came out to see us play or practice for the first time, you may have said to yourself, "That boy ain't quite right."

OK, let's get this out of the way right now. I never hit a player (*damn laws*), I never made personal attacks on them (*damn lawyers*), nor have I ever *deliberately* publicly embarrassed a player (but I know it happened and I regret that).

For the most part, I enjoyed a great rapport with my players —and I am blessed that many of them continue to be a big part of my life. I love every one of them, and most of them love their old coach (and even the ones that don't love me, do not hate me). So, please read this entire chapter before organizing the intervention. Besides, I am retired.

I held my players to very high standards on the street, in the classroom, and on the field. I truly believe that the first step to becoming a champion is to walk, talk, and act like a champion at all times. And, if anyone fails to do their dead-level best to comply, they should have to answer for it. It's as simple as that.

When I was upset, I let my players know it and we settled it right then and there. Then, we would move on. Once we settled an issue, it was hardly ever brought back up (unless in jest). *I hate it when old, settled issues are brought back up. If it's settled, then it's settled. Let it go and move on.*

Although society was continually lowering the standard of what is considered *average* or *normal*, I was not willing to stand by and allow any of my kids to strive to be average at anything. In today's world that is too easy. Average has become more or less a synonym for *underachievement*. I do not have any interest in working with anyone who can live with being average. I talked openly to my players about average and I challenged them to strive for *greatness*, to yearn to walk among the *elite*. I begged them to never be satisfied with the notion of being average at anything.

If one of my players goes on to be a janitor at the zoo, I want her to want to be the best damn janitor the zoo has ever had. When all the other janitors sit around talking, I would want my former player to be the janitor to whom they compare themselves. I would never want one of my former players to be a mere average janitor. (I would like to think that I could have at least produced *above average janitors* from within our program.)

If you were to ask any of my former players:

- "Was Scott Whitlock demanding?" the reply would be "Yes."
- "Was he tough to play for?" they'd say, "Oh yeah."
- "Did he push you to the limits?" most would say "Very much so."

I would consider all those answers to be both accurate and fair.

Then ask them:

- "If you had an emergency and could not reach a family member, who could you call?" A majority would list Scott Whitlock within their answer—I may not be number one, but I'd be on the list. Why? They trust me and know they can count on me.
- "Why do you trust that tall, baldheaded redneck who constantly rode herd on you?" Most would say, "Because, from the day a player entered the KSU program, Coach Whitlock made a conscious effort to earn our trust, to teach us that our lives and futures are important to him. And, he strived to show us that we matter to him."

My players always knew where they stood with me and they knew I would stand by them through thick and thin—and I still do. In my eyes, that's the only way it can be. A coach and team are so interdependent upon each other. *Trust* must be established early and maintained daily.

If you cannot truly *trust* the people with whom you work, then productivity will be affected. Over the years, for the most part, I had the *trust* of my players. Without it, I would not have won nearly as many games as I did.

By having their *trust*, I was afforded the opportunity to push them to their *limits*. I attempted to get each player I coached to seek out exactly what their limits really were. In different ways, I constantly asked them, "How good are you? How good can you be?"

I believe that most players come to the collegiate game believing that their potential and limits are significantly less than they actually are. So I was willing to push, pull, kick, or anything else I had to do in an effort to get my players to seek and reach their full potential. My players would have never allowed me to do this if I they had not trusted me.

From day one, each player knew I would never compare them to anything or anyone else. I only measured them against my evaluation and perception of what they could become on the street, in the classroom, or on the field. At every practice and on every game day, I demanded *everything* from each of our players. Also, each day I attempted to have an actual conversation with each player on our squad. It may have been brief, it may have been trivial, but I wanted each kid to know that I knew they were there and they were an important part of my life.

As I said, my tactics were sometimes misunderstood by those unfamiliar with me. I can understand that. To see me at practice or on game day for the first time, one could easily have been taken aback by my bluntness and the confrontational demeanor I showed at times. I am blessed and cursed with a loud speaking voice, so when I speak, a lot of people hear me. When I was speaking to a player on the field, especially if it was an unpleasant chat, bystanders at times heard perhaps more than they should have. In reflection, *I hate that*. I will admit, the years made me smarter and milder. By the end of my coaching career, I did not allow loud episodes to happen as often as they once did. That being said, looking back, they still likely occurred too often. Thankfully, my players *got it*. They understood what I was trying to do and *they trusted me*. It was all based on trust.

My rants and ravings on the field were intended to prompt my players to grow and improve; however, they were often mistaken for me simply being an *ass*. Now, whether I am or was an *ass* or not, depends upon with whom you speak; but never should you confuse my delivery style with my message. Everything I did, even when I failed, was done with the intentions of making us better.

I was a tough critic of my players, but I was also their biggest fan. I remain blood loyal to my girls. During our years together on the field, I may have yelled at them and they may have gotten mad me, but if anyone else would have gotten in any of our faces, that poor soul would have to deal with both the players and the coach. I do not know why, but it was always that way between my players and me.

My players knew me—they still know me. Our fans knew me, (most of) our parents knew me. Unfortunately, someone (perhaps seeing us for the first time) may have not. One of the funniest cases of a fan (of an opponent) misunderstanding *what I was up to* happened in Valdosta, Georgia, in 1993. Here's how it went down:

We were in Valdosta playing in a midseason tournament. We were playing a school from Florida (I cannot remember which). We got out in front early and by the third inning, we were up 19-0. When I say, "we got in front early," I am being nice. Our opponent was horrible. They could not catch nor throw, and they surely could not hit. With such a lead, I took the liberty of clearing my bench and giving some of my younger players playing time.

This is a good time to make a point. It was clear we were not going to lose that game. I could have just sat back and yucked it up as the innings melted away, but I did not. I knew I had a new set of players in the game and this was their time to play and learn, so I continued to *coach 'em hard.* We were not going to steal or bunt or do anything to run up the score, but I wanted the kids in the lineup to play hard, to be fundamentally sound, and to respect the game.

At one point, our team made errors on three consecutive at bats. After the third, I had had enough. I barked for time, proceeded to stomp to the mound and summoned all nine players. Once they assembled, I lit into them with no reservations. I told them how they were looking and that they should not be satisfied to win a game that was won before they entered the lineup. I was fairly terse and quite loud. I then returned to the dugout.

When we retired the side and I went over from our first base dugout to coach third, I was getting an earful from our opponent's fans. At one point, one of their fans made his way down to the fence. Once there, he repeatedly chirped, "Hey coach, hey coach." I tried to ignore it but finally between the first and second batter, I caved. "WHAT?" I replied. He then snorted, "I just wanted you to know that I can't believe that you'd give your kids grief when you're up nearly 20 runs. You're a disgrace. My daughter would never play for you!" *Sometimes they make it too easy for me.*

I asked the man, "Is your kid on this team (as I pointed to the team which was in the field)?" He snapped, "Yeah, what about it?" I repeated, "You mean this team here (as I again pointed)?" "YES!" he said. I then ended our brief chat by agreeing with him, *"Mister, you are 100 percent right! If she's on THAT team, she would never play for me."*

With smoke pouring from the back of his trousers, he stomped back to his seat—after suggesting that I was the product of some sacrilegious tryst between my dad and a horse. He had gotten my point.

Early in my career, I asked Georgia State University's Head Softball Coach Bob Heck (a Georgia collegiate coaching treasure) for his insight on recruiting. He spoke about many things, but what I remember most from that conversation is when he said, *"I cannot coach a kid that I cannot pull for."*

For the most part, I feel the same way. I have no interest in working with any player in which I did not believe. My players and I spent the better part of 10 months of the year together. By being fond of and pulling for the people with which I work was the only way I could have maintained my sanity (such as it is).

Some people may not believe that I pulled for every kid with which I ever worked—especially if they saw us play (or me at work) only once. Those who know me, and more importantly, those who played for me are fully aware of my respect and appreciation for them.

I am not saying that my *style* of coaching was the best approach. I am not even saying that what I did is even really a style at all. I certainly do not recommend it when working with today's athletes. I am just stating that my type of *old school* and *in-your-face coaching* was the way that worked for me back in the day.

I have no idea as to why, but during all my years in the game, I was able to find players that bought into it and I owe them so much.

Owls win!

15

DYAN SETS ME STRAIGHT

I have learned many things from many people over my career. Some of my best teachers have been my players. On a spring day in 1992, I was taught a great lesson by a pitcher from Calgary, Alberta, Canada. Her name is Dyan "Dy" Mueller.

Dyan was the first real star player we had at Kennesaw. When we were in the process of building our first team, my then-assistant Don McKinlay, a Canada native, told me an old baseball teammate of his had a sister who pitched up in Alberta. My first instinct was "Great, Don's buddy's sister needs a scholarship. Now how am I going to get out of this one?" I told Don to get me a tape of her and I'd take a look.

I had low, if any, expectations of what I'd see when the tape arrived. When it came in, to my surprise, she was pretty darn good. She seemed to have a few pitches and could hit a little bit. So, we signed Dyan Mueller to a scholarship.

When Dy arrived in the fall of 1990, she joined a roster made up of a coaching staff that had never seen a complete fastpitch game played, 11 teammates who had never played fastpitch in their lives and three other recruited fastpitch players. Yes sir, Kennesaw State fastpitch softball was open for business.

I quickly learned a couple of things about Dyan. First, she is blessed with a great, dry sense of humor. Secondly, when it was time to work she was all business. While at KSU, she took her academics very seriously, had an ideal work ethic for an athlete, and seemingly never got rattled! She quickly became the squad's leader.

Our first year was truly a Cinderella season. Our little group put together a 41-11 record and finish fourth nationally. No one was more surprised than we were.

Going into season two (1992) the team was carrying momentum. We had an excellent recruiting class and were talented. The glaring weaknesses the team had were *depth at pitching* and a *coach who did not exhibit patience (and who did not know when to shut up).*

During the second game of a home doubleheader in the 1992 season, Dyan Mueller gave me one of the finest lessons I have learned while coaching—it had to do a lot with that no patience and big mouth thing I just mentioned.

Here's what happened:

The 1992 team was talented. We had a star pitcher in Dyan, a future Olympian behind the plate (Colleen Thorburn) and four future All-Americans in other positions. We were sailing through the regular season, so I felt I needed to keep a *firm hold to the reigns* and not let the club get too cocky. I would find the smallest thing and go ballistic over it. I would rant and rave and I would go out of my way to tear apart the confidence of this talented group of players. What an idiot I was!

Due to my rants the team was an emotional wreck. Every player, that is, except the stoic Dyan Mueller. Any rant toward her direction would bead up and fall off her like rain falling off a waxed car. In reflection, I feel Dy knew even though my approach was wrong, I was trying to push/pull us back to the national tournament. Either that, or she knew that I was an inexperienced coach who's just full of s***. I choose to believe the former, but the latter is probably closer to the truth.

We were up 5-1 in the top of the sixth inning against Georgia College with Dy on the mound. With one out, no one on base, and an 0 and 2 count on the hitter, bingo, a single to left. "Dyan keep your damn head in the game," I barked from the dugout. She gave me a glare that still gives me chills.

Now, all softball coaches (not just us morons) hate 0 and 2 base hits. In fact, most coaches feel that if a pitcher is up no balls and two strikes on a batter and then gives up a hit, it should be legal to have the pitcher immediately imprisoned so they can reflect upon their heinous act (a belief I still support).

The very next hitter came up with one out and one on. Dy quickly got out to an 0 and 2 count and then BANG—a single to right.

Before the right fielder had thrown the ball to her cutoff person, I had screamed "Time!" and began marching to the mound. Dy simply stood there staring at me. I waved off all the infielders. This conversation was to be between my pitcher, my catcher, and me.

Dyan Mueller: What a competitor

* * *

Colleen Thorburn, who at that time was a fine freshman catcher, was nearly trembling when she got to the mound. I was clearly shaking, and Dyan was there with a *what the hell are you doing here* look on her face. I spouted, "Dyan could you please tell me, what in THE hell is going on out here?" With all the coolness of a cat burglar she said, "Coach, in both cases Colleen gave a signal, I acknowledged, and pitched. And in both cases, the ball did not end up in the location that I had intended. You are just going to have to live with that!"

Colleen, though she tried not to, started to smile, Dyan looked at me for a reply and I said, "Well all right then." Then I walked away. I returned to the dugout enlightened and with a little less pride. As I entered our dugout area, I gathered myself enough to answer a question offered by my assistant coach, "What did you say to her coach?" I replied, "I told her to get her head out of her ass and focus." *Dyan may have put me in my place, but I was not going to admit it to him.*

As I remember, Dyan struck out the next two hitters to end the inning. In less than five sentences, Dyan had taught me quite the lesson. With those few words, she conveyed to me, *"Hey, Coach, guess what. Players do not intend to screw up, and they too have pride. And no amount of yelling is going to undo a mistake."*

16

BE CAREFUL OF WHAT YOU ASK—THEY JUST MIGHT ANSWER YOU

We should take questions more seriously. If we would just think about what we are asking and to whom we are asking it, we could save ourselves a lot of time and embarrassment. I have concluded that Congress should pass a bill that requires everyone to stop and think before asking any question. I also believe that if one asks an ill-timed, bad, or stupid question then one deserves whatever one gets. It has happened to all of us. At one time or another, everybody has had the misfortune of asking a question that has gotten them into a situation or a conversation they regret.

Just think of some of the dangerous little questions that we ask each day, "How ya' doing?"; "Where ya' going?"; "What's going on?"; "How ya' feeling?" One would think that these little questions would be safe and harmless. They are regularly offered as simple salutations—*with no expectations of a real response.* I mean, if I pass someone in the hall and say, "How, ya' doing?"—the last thing I want them to do is to *really* tell me how they are actually doing. In fact, I would rather they just grunt or not even reply so I could just keep walking. However, because I have the habit of saying "How ya' doing?" I run the risk of having to actually learn things about people I do not need to know. When I open the door and ask things like, "How ya' doing?" I rarely consider the peril involved in such questions, but I should.

You would think that I'd learn to not ask certain things, but yet, I have not. I still do it, you still do it, we all still do it. Let me give you a couple of examples of what has happened to me when I have chosen to roll the dice and ask questions without first thinking.

One of my former players has a mom who is never happy unless she is unhappy. This woman always has something that hurts or something bothering her. It was no secret, everyone knew it, but since I only saw the lady on game days (and from a distance) her quirks meant very little to me —until...

One afternoon, after a game, I was walking to the parking lot to get into my truck and go home. On my way, I happened past the *Queen of Whines*. In a complete lapse of my senses I offered a question that was not well thought out and one in which I surely did not want a reply. "How are things going Ms. X?" For the next 30 minutes, I found out.

Her son was "doing pot" (I assume she meant smoking it), she just had two corns removed, her shoes hurt, she didn't like her daughter's boyfriend, her mother's gallbladder was bad, and her husband smokes too much and is "going to catch the cancer." I mean if it was happening in her life, I was brought up to speed on it. When I finally concluded that I had no immediate means of committing suicide or murder, I finally mustered the courage just to say, "I've really got to go now," and she walked away.

As I scooped up what was left of my central nervous system from the asphalt and crawled into my truck, I asked several *well thought out* questions of myself, "Nice job dumbass, you just had to ask—didn't ya'?" "What were you thinking?" "Is there anyone stupider than you?" The answers that I came to were: "Yep." "I wasn't." "There can't be."

Coaches can run into unnecessary difficulties, if they ask certain questions of their players at the wrong time. Communication is vital to any team's success. However, there are times that a coach should just trust his/her own good judgment, believe in his/her players, and *just not ask certain questions*. Fore if you *ask*, they just might answer, and you might not be prepared for what you hear. This brings me to my stupid question number two...

I never coached a harder working player than Carol Ann Orsak Walker. She wasn't the fastest, the strongest, or the best hitter, but she *brought it* to the park every day. We could always depend on Carol to work as hard as she could and to give it her best to make the team go. If I had only remembered that one certain day, I could have saved myself a ton of embarrassment.

During a 1991 practice, we were in the midst of working on team defense. We were doing a relay drill and had defenders in all nine positions. The remaining players were being utilized as base runners. Everybody was around—players, coaches, managers—and could easily see and hear everything that was taking place.

Somewhere in the drill, I hit a routine fly ball out to Carol who was positioned in left field. It was an easy enough ball to handle and I was shocked when she did not make her usual effort to catch it on the fly. She just jogged over and picked it up (after it had hit the ground) and tossed it in to the shortstop. At first, I was not sure I had seen what I thought I just saw. Anyone who knows me—especially those who play or have played for me—knows my views and reactions towards people who do not hustle or work hard. So, I really could not believe that Carol had just loafed in a drill—it was so out of character for her.

I immediately hit another fly ball to her. Again, the same results. I turned to my then-assistant, Don McKinlay and asked,

"What the hell was that?" He shrugged. Don has great instincts and could easily sense what was about to happen and immediately took precautionary measures. He went and stood behind a screen.

When I hit the third ball out past Carol, I was already standing by the shortstop as she finished *jogging* to pick it up. It was from that location that I asked my poorly thought out question.

"Carol, what in the hell is wrong with you?" Without missing a beat, she put both hands on her hip and yelled, *"Coach, I don't feel good. That's all I've got today! OK?"*

Well, I was not going to stand for that, so I did what any semi-intelligent male that coaches women for a living would do in that situation. I shouted "OK, I'm sorry," and went back to the plate and did not hit another ball near left field for the next two days.

The fly ball incident with Carol reminded me of several things that a coach should never forget:

1. **Communication is the key:** I should have asked Carol as to the situation after the first ball and not tried to make an example of her; **OR**, she could have made me aware of her *limitations* that particular day. If either had occurred, I would not have asked that stupid question.
2. **Believe in your players:** I knew Carol Orsak was a hard worker, and my first thought should not have been that she was loafing.
3. **Never mess with a crabby left fielder!**

17

YOU CAN LEARN A LOT SITTING ON WOODEN BENCHES

The 1995 season was KSU's first as a member of the NCAA. Although we had enjoyed success in our four years within the NAIA, nobody really knew where we'd shake out when going up against programs at the *next level*. As you can imagine, everyone was ecstatic when we won that year's Division II National Championship. The ride was amazing. Even more amazing were the players. The 1995 team was a team of character and dedication. The players were hungry as were their coaches.

In our program's first four seasons (1991-94), we had three fourth-place and one national runner-up finishes. Four seasons, four top four finishes. Yet, nearly anywhere one of us went someone would ask, "Do you think that y'all will ever win the *big one*?"

Isn't it funny, usually the people who ask stupid questions like that are folks who have never accomplished one thing in their entire lives? They usually were the last ones picked when the kids chose teams or have a job they hate. Then, in attempt to make themselves feel better, they seem to get great joy in pointing out the shortcomings of others. I do not fully understand that. I guess, when one has done absolutely nothing of significance, it makes them feel better when they try to convince others that they too are failures.

We were not failures—*far from it*. Our program had finished in the top four in each of its first four years of existence and yet, we had to constantly defend ourselves. Looking back, I find that silly, but at the time, it really hurt—both players and coaches. When we finally *rang the bell* in 1995, it was most satisfying to each of us. We were happy for ourselves, the Kennesaw State family, and for all former players from each of our first four teams.

During the Kennesaw State softball's 2005 season, we held a 10-year reunion event to honor the 1995 National Championship team. It was great. Fifteen of the 18 players from that squad returned as did former coaches, invited fans, and boosters. We spent three hours having dinner, reminiscing, laughing, and crying. It was a conversation during the reunion that inspired me to write this chapter. The chat was between Candi Cain (a senior on the 1995 team) and yours truly.

The circumstances surrounding the end of Candi's senior season is a story worth telling. She clearly demonstrated strength and character. The situation she found herself in also speaks to the difficult choices coaches sometimes face. She is also an example of how an athlete can and should handle a tough situation.

Candi Cain was our starting second baseman for our first 49 games in 1995. She was a hard worker, a hustler, and an excellent student. She never got into trouble and was a caring teammate. Throughout our '95 regular season, Candi had ups and downs at the plate and had a few struggles in the field. Though I had concerns, I chose to stick with her as our second baseman for the entire 1995 regular season and conference tournament.

After our conference tourney, I was unsatisfied with our team's defensive consistency. After looking at every possibility and weighing my options, I made the decision to *sit* Candi and move another player to second. The decision was (and still is) the hardest decision I have ever made in 28 years of coaching.

Once the move was made, Candi Cain showed the world her true character. A lesser person might have quit and walked away, but not Candi. Each day she continued to come to the ballpark and work hard. She continued to be the consummate teammate. Even though she might have disagreed with my move, she continued to support her head coach. I still use her attitude throughout that ordeal as an example to this day. When we won the national championship in 1995, Candi was as happy as anyone. She's really quite a person.

As our reunion began to wind down, several of us found ourselves in the lobby of Kennesaw State's new baseball and softball field house—the Bobbie Bailey Athletic Complex. As we stood in the lobby, Candi made the remark, "Coach, you have got to be proud of this building. You have just got to be proud."

The Bobbie Bailey Athletic Complex (KSU softball's current home) is one of the finest facilities around and is very different from the facility on which Candi and her teammates had played. When Candi's career at Kennesaw State began, her (and her teammates') locker room was their cars, their team room was the library, there was no weight room at the field, and the training room was a quarter of a mile away back in the gym. When *nature called*, there were two choices. The first was the woods across the street. The second was to attempt to set a record for self-discipline. When a run was scored, one of our non-starters would hang the tally on our manual scoreboard. The dugouts consisted of two pine benches and a few concrete blocks. Our outfield fence was made of plastic and would blow down regularly. Chalked lines separated *in play* from *out of play*. The field wasn't much to see.

No one ever complained—except me. Daily, the players

would show up and work hard on getting better. Nothing was given to them. They worked for everything they received. If the fence needed repairing, they did it. If the field needed raking, they went and got the rakes. On cold drizzly days, we all got wet and shivered. That's the way it was. By the time Candi's group were seniors, we did have dugouts and the pines had been replaced by a Port-O-Let. Other than that, nearly everything else was the same.

I have always felt that the players of that era, due partly to what they had to endure, were tougher and hungrier than those of today. The 1995 players' work ethic was beyond reproach. Their record speaks for itself. It was a great time to coach softball in Kennesaw, Georgia.

I'm sorry for straying. I'll get back to Candi's and my conversation during the reunion. As I said, while we stood among the others in the lobby as our reunion was ending, Candi said to me, "Coach, you have got to be proud of this building. You have just got to be proud." I said, "Yeah, it is great. I owe it all to you guys. Your teams are the ones that built this place. I just wish that it had been here for y'all to enjoy. Don't you?"

She quickly replied, "Nope, I would not change a thing about what we did and went through in those days." "You really wouldn't?" I asked. "NO! Definitely not," she said. Then I asked her, "Why?"

She ended our chat by saying, *"Coach, we learned a lot sittin' on those old wooden benches."*

By profession, Candi is a schoolteacher and coach. When we had our chat back in 2005, her quote regarding learning and wooden benches didn't really register with me, but as I started collecting my thoughts about doing this book, Candi's statement flashed back into my forethought.

There is so much in what she said. Whereas I do not know if she had a particular lesson that she learned in mind, I do know that there are many things all of us could have learned on those benches. After pondering all the lessons we learned, I believe that I have identified the most important.

If you surround yourself with quality people, if you trust one another, and if you stick together, it does not matter where or upon what you sit. You will be successful, and what's more, you will be glad that you were a part of what happened.

Thanks for the lesson Candi.

18

DAWG FOR A DAY

I am a college football nut, I always have been. The distance from the home in which I was reared in Bostwick, Georgia, to the seats in Sanford Stadium in Athens, Georgia, is approximately 20 miles. Sanford Stadium is the home of the University of Georgia's football team.

I, like most from my area—*except John Ruark, who loved Bear Bryant and Alabama*—grew up a UGA fan. As a Bulldog or a *Dawg (if you are classy enough to utilize appropriate nomenclature)* football fan during the 1960s and '70s, there were three constants:

1. **Vince Dooley was always the head football coach.** He is a legendary coach, athletic administrator, and state treasure. He led the entire UGA athletic program to heights never seen in the Classic City prior to his arrival. He always kidded about being a "poor mouther" because he always paid any upcoming opponent great respect—even bad ones. I am not going to go as far as to use the term "poor mouth," but I did once hear him comment on a much lesser opponent's long snapper (*the player that hikes the ball for punts and field goals*).

After hearing that, even the biggest fan of Coach Dooley would have to admit that one who lauds an opponent's long snapper could be viewed as someone who looks hard for something positive to say about another team.

2. **Larry Munson was the radio voice of the Dawgs.** What made him great is that he was a *homer*. There was no neutrality within his presentation. He anguished over victory or defeat for every second of every game. You were exhausted after listening to him. He was the greatest. If you do not believe me, just go to YouTube, punch in his name and listen.

3. **Sanford Stadium was THE PLACE TO BE for five or six Saturday afternoons (*the stadium had no lights back then*) each autumn.** For someone who attended Georgia or grew up being a Dawg fan, there is still nothing like it.

I feel that these three pieces of information are important for you to know before you read any more of this chapter.

May of 2000

We lost in the national championship finals to a great North Dakota State team in 2000. The 2000 season was our 10th for fastpitch softball at Kennesaw State. During our first decade, we won two NCAA Division II National Championships, had been national runners-up twice, and had advanced to our College World Series in nine of our 10 seasons. We, as a program, were red hot.

In the mid-1990s, UGA athletics, under the leadership of Director of Athletics Vince Dooley (*the legendary football coach became Georgia's AD in 1979 and held that position until 2004*), like many schools within the Southeastern Conference, added fastpitch to their roster of intercollegiate sports. UGA's first several seasons playing fastpitch were average at best. At the conclusion of the 2000 season, they decided to make a coaching change.

When I learned of the potential opening at Georgia, I was very interested. *Home. Georgia. Division I. Dream job. Wow.* Once the opening became official, I immediately notified KSU's Athletic Director, Dr. Dave Waples, that I was going to apply. He understood and was supportive. I applied.

Unbeknownst to me, I was on the radar of Georgia's athletic administration. They foresaw that they would be making a change and began forming a "short list" early in the 2000 season. Apparently, I was among their potential candidates. Coach Lewis Gainey, UGA's legendary track coach and administrator, was chairing the softball search. Again, unbeknownst to me, Coach Gainey and another committee member came and watched us play in the 2000 World Series. I am glad I did not know that. Back in 2000, I would have likely soiled myself two or three times per game if I had known that the Dawgs were scouting me.

At the conclusion of the 2000 World Series, Coach Gainey let me know that they were considering me. I assured him of my interest and that I would welcome a chance to interview. A few days later, my wife Susan, my dear friends Ernie and Carolee White, and I flew to Chicago for a mini-vacation to see the sites and to take in a Cub's game. Luckily, the Cub's game was early in the trip.

On day three of the five-day trip (the morning after the Cubs game), I got a call from Coach Gainey. "Scott, Vince wants to meet you and he's leaving town in two days for a week. How soon can you come over?" After hearing the words "Vince," "meet," and "you," I went numb. I quickly surmised that "Vince" meant **Coach Vince Dooley**, but for several minutes, I had trouble with the "meet" and "you" parts.

In May of 2000, for a college softball coach from Bostwick, Georgia, that had listened to Larry Munson all his life to hear that Vince Dooley wants an audience was about as big as it got. It was also terrifying.

Without having any idea of how I was going to do it, I told Coach Gainey, "I am in Chicago on vacation with my wife and friends. I'll be there in the morning." We quickly went about getting me on a flight for Atlanta later that day. I left Susan, Ernie, and Carolee in Chi-Town and headed home—not to our Marietta home, but I mean *home* (so I thought).

Once home, I found my black suit and a red tie. I then began to put together my thoughts and a small presentation for the search committee. I was so nervous that I barely slept. The next morning, I scatted down GA 316 to Athens and to the Butts-Mehre Building—the home of UGA's athletic administration. Once there, Coach Gainey gave me a tour of Butts-Mehre and then proceeded to walk me around a place that was so special to me.

Athens was the nearest *real city* to my hometown, so I was very familiar with Stegeman Coliseum—where I parked for football game days—and all the surroundings.

I had not been on a job interview in 16 years, so as we walked, I kept telling myself, "Stay calm, he would not be doing all this if you were not an actual option for them."

Eventually we made our way back to Butts-Mehre and I met with the selection committee. As our meeting went along, a door on the opposite end of the room from where I sat opened and Coach Dooley walked in. "I just wanted to stop in and meet you. I look forward to visiting with you a little later." He shook my hand and then left the room. I think that I responded to his greeting, but I got *big eyed* at seeing him and I honestly do not remember what I said—if anything.

After regaining my senses, we finished what must have been a great meeting with the search committee. Then, Coach Gainey and a few others took me to lunch. During lunch, I got the sense that I was more than just one of the candidates. The questions and comments made me feel as if I had a great chance at the job.

As we drove back to campus after lunch, Coach Gainey said to me, "After you get done with Vince, we'll take you out to see the construction site of the new softball/soccer complex." *New complex? Now we're talkin'!* Then I realized that I was about to meet one-on-one with one of the NCAA's most respected and powerful administrators, who also was a legend in our state. He was someone that, *with the snap of his fingers,* could give me my dream job (so I thought). I became very nervous. No, I was scared to death.

When his administrative assistant said to me, "Coach, you can go on in, he's ready for you," my legs did not immediately want to leave the chair in which I sat. However, after a brief second, I managed to get up and go. "Scott, thank you for coming down. I hear that you were in Chicago yesterday." I replied, "Yes sir, and my wife still is." He laughed and that helped settle me down.

As we talked, he painted a picture of what he wanted for softball at Georgia and I tried to relate as to how I would go about it. We met for about 20 minutes. He then asked Coach Gainey to join us. Coach Dooley asked Coach Gainey to have someone drive me over to see the building site. He explained, "I am short on time and need to talk with Coach Gainey." Therefore, a very nice woman took me over to see the construction site of what is now UGA's softball stadium. It was about a 10-minute drive over, we looked around for about 15 minutes, and drove 10 minutes back.

When we re-entered the athletic offices, Coach Gainey took me back to Coach Dooley. Coach Dooley asked me directly, "Would you like this job?" I said, "Yes sir!" He replied, "Great. Lewis take him over to see Damon (Evans) and talk about a contract. Scott, I hate to cut this short, but I have got to run." I nodded (I do not recall speaking).

Just that fast, Vince Dooley offered me the opportunity to become the University of Georgia's head softball coach. My head was spinning.

Coach Gainey and I then went two offices over for me to meet with Damon Evans who was their CFO at the time. Damon and I visited and talked about the terms of a four-year contract. We shook hands. As the meeting ended, I remember telling Coach Gainey and Damon how excited I was about getting a shot at my dream job, but "I needed to talk with Susan (who was returning home from Chicago that night) before I signed anything." Of course, they understood.

I pulled out of Athens floating on air that afternoon. From Bostwick to Kennesaw to Athens, I simply could not believe it. On my drive home, I called Susan, who had returned from Chicago, about the day's events. When she answered, I said, "Honey, I think we're moving." She was excited about it. After chatting only a few minutes, I told her that I needed to call Dr. Waples (KSU's AD) and my mom and dad.

I had deliberately kept my dad, the late Bobby Whitlock, in the dark about any possibilities of me becoming a coach at the University of Georgia. I had to do that in order to keep my sanity. If I had told my dad that any of the UGA process was taking place, he would have driven me crazy. He was an over-the-top Bulldog fan whose home was only 20 minutes from Athens. Had he known that my name was in the running for the gig, he would have hired private eyes to dig up dirt on all other candidates. If he had known that I was actually interviewing for the job, he would have wanted to go on the interview for me.

Do not be misled, any reaction or actions that my dad might have taken (upon hearing my news) would not have been due to his fervent interest in his son's softball career. He would have been angling from jumpstart for only one thing—FOOTBALL TICKETS!

After hanging up with Susan, I immediately called Dr. Waples. He was supportive. I told him about the salary offer and he knew my love of the Dawgs. He congratulated and told me, "I'll call the president (KSU's President, Dr. Betty Siegel) and I'll see you tomorrow."

As I stated, after speaking with Dr. Waples, I called my mom. She was happy. I then called my dad. "What? Why didn't you tell me that this was going on?" was his immediate response. Before he said anything about "congratulations" or being "happy for me," he asked two additional questions in this order: "Football tickets are part of your package, right? "What kind of salary did you get?" He eventually got around to telling me he was proud of "us." *You cannot make stuff like that up.*

I made one final call on my way home. I called my assistant coach and right arm, Don McKinlay. When he answered, I asked him, "Wanna move to Athens, Donny? He quickly gave me a "Hell yeah."

There is no way that I would have considered taking on the UGA job without Don. As I have often said, "Had there been no Don McKinlay, there would have been no Scott Whitlock." He was the lightening to my thunder. He is one of the finest people that I know, and I owe him so much.

After five calls and about two hours of driving, I made it home. When I came into the house from the garage, Susan greeted me with a hug and a piece of paper. "What's this?" I asked. She told me it was Dr. Siegel's home telephone number and that she wanted me to call her immediately. I did. As I dialed her number, I thought that I was calling to get a "congrats" from KSU's president. I was wrong.

When she answered, I barely got, "Hi Dr. Siegel, its Sco..." out of my mouth before she yelled, "Did you sign anything today?" "No ma'am," I replied. "Good. Are you willing to come up and visit with me tomorrow morning?" I quickly said, "Dr. Siegel, of course. After 15 years of working for you, you know I will." She said, "Eight o'clock OK?" "Yes ma'am." She then made one request, and that simple assignment shaped and solidified the remainder of my life. Dr. Siegel said, "**Between now and then, I want you to make me a list of what I have to do to keep you.**" "Yes ma'am, I will."

Her request at the end of our chat sparked a feeling in my gut that eventually led to changing the way I look at my profession and happiness itself.

When I hung up the phone, I told Susan what she had said. Her response was, "How about that?" How about that indeed. After chatting with Susan, I began to make *my list.* I had no real expectations that Kennesaw State would be willing or able to do anything that would change my mind. Then a funny thing happened. As I worked on the requested list, Dr. Siegel's question (*and the sincerity I felt as she said it*) kept rattling in my head. After giving it my best efforts, I only had four items on my list. After finishing it, all I wanted to do was go to sleep. I was exhausted, but once in bed I could not sleep.

My day had been crazy. Between getting up and going to bed, I had interviewed for my *dream job,* been offered it, and had tentatively accepted it. I had notified my boss, assistant coach, and family that I was going to leave KSU for Georgia. I had also promised a mentor that I'd at least meet with her before I went and chased my career's dream. I was somewhat numb as I finally dozed off. The next morning came quickly. I was dreading to tell Dr. Siegel that I was leaving. I knew that I would need to contact the KSU players and was convinced that it was going to be a tough day.

When the elevator door opened on the fifth floor of Kennesaw Hall, Dr. Siegel was actually walking in the hallway from her office towards her suite's reception area. She walked directly up to me and said, "You're coming to tell me goodbye, aren't you?" I quickly told her (and I meant it), "No, Miss Betty. I came to talk to my boss about my opportunity, get her thoughts." We then walked to her office. After she shut the door, she asked if I had made my list. I told her that I had. She said, "OK, let's go." I said, "All right." The first item on my list was the salary UGA offered. *The number was so much more than my current salary, I just knew that it would end our chat.*

When I gave her the number and asked if KSU could match it, she answered in one word, "**DONE.**" I nearly fainted. The speed in which she gave me her answer almost frightened me. I then asked if it was possible for me to be relieved of all my "other duties" and solely coach softball.

In 2000 at Kennesaw State, necessity dictated that coaches perform auxiliary duties to help with their salaries and make the place go. At the time, I was the coordinator for all athletic summer camps on campus. KSU's College of Professional Education *owned and administered* summer camps, but we coaches were paid to run them. It was a prickly topic among us coaches to say the least.

Camp coordinator was only one of the auxiliary duties I performed during my time at KSU. From 1989-1995, I was our sports information director, but I resigned from that position immediately after writing the story reporting my 1995 team winning the national championship (Remember that Dr. Waples? Ha!). I have also been an assistant compliance officer, an assistant women's basketball coach, and bus driver. Lastly, I had to listen to Dave Waples' jokes for 24 years. After hearing my request for relief of "other duties," Dr. Siegel's response was, "**DONE.**"

My third request was for Dr. Siegel to instruct Professional Education that "ownership" of athletic summer camps be moved to Athletics' control so that all coaches could have an opportunity to make more money annually. "**DONE.**" By that point, my emotions and thoughts were swirling. I was amazed and so grateful for the way Dr. Siegel was responding to my requests.

The last item on my list was for help raising interest and funds to build a baseball/softball facility. (In 2000 the KSU's baseball and softball team had nice fields. However, the challenges were the coaches' offices located near the gym, neither team had locker rooms, and many game day amenities were temporary structures.) "DONE."

As strange as this may sound, before the "un" sound in the word "done" came from Betty Siegel's mouth for the fourth time in five minutes, I knew that I had been wrong all along. I thought that the UGA job was an opportunity for me to chase a dream and go home. Over the course of 300 seconds, I learned that I had been home for 15 years and that I was already living my dream. I was a head coach at a fine university that wanted Scott Whitlock.

Me, Rhubarb, and Dr. Siegel

UGA was a university in the market for a softball coach. They felt that I was qualified and offered me a chance to take a crack at it. The fact that the name was Scott Whitlock was incidental when it came to their offer. The folks at KSU knew Scott Whitlock, warts and all, and they wanted me to stay. The president of Kennesaw State taught me what it means to be *wanted*. It remains a career highlight.

After the fourth "**DONE**" and my epiphany, I swallowed and said, "Dr. Siegel, if I can just have something in writing about all this later today, I will withdraw from the Georgia job." She jumped up and hugged me. *For the record, I had that agreement in writing within 30 minutes of that hug.* And, that was that.

From that moment on, I was "**DONE**" with thinking about other jobs or chasing dreams. I knew that I was *home*. I walked, on a cloud, back to our offices. As I often do when making professional decisions, I called *The King* (my friend, Mike Candrea) to double-check myself and to get his take. Once I told him of my conversation with Dr. Siegel and how my insides were feeling, he said, "If you are happy, then you would be a fool to leave Kennesaw." The call ended (*of course it was 6 a.m. in Casa Grande, Arizona when I phoned, so I respected his brevity*).

When I told Dr. Waples I was staying, as well as about being "relieved" of my camp duties and how Athletics now "owned" summer athletic camps, he shook my hand and immediately griped about the money. He also lamented that I had likely just got Mike Sansing (KSU's baseball coach and my dear friend) a raise, too. He was right. I went to Susan's office to tell her. She was excited for me.

I called Coach Gainey at Georgia and told him of my decision. He was very classy about it. Coach Dooley was too and *he even called from his road trip to congratulate me.* Georgia went on to hire Lu Harris who is still enjoying a legendary career leading the Dawgs softball team.

In the end, it was a huge win-win for both Georgia and Scott Whitlock. UGA got the quality softball coach for which they were seeking and I ended up with my dream job.

After learning that he had no free football tickets headed his way, my daddy took it as expected. It only took three years for him to speak to me again. Thank the Lord that we had a distant cousin die and we ended up at the same funeral otherwise we may have never spoken again. I guess a death in the family made him realize that there might be a few (but only a few) things more important than Georgia football season tickets.

To this day people will ask me if I regret not taking the Georgia job. My answer is always the same, "Not one bit. I'm home."

God bless Betty Siegel for opening my eyes. Go Dawgs and *GO OWLS!*

19

"WHAT A LITTLE OLE FIVE-GAME WINNING STREAK CAN DO."

The 1995 softball season changed my life, but before I delve into that there are some things you need to know.

To say the least, my career has been eventful. I have been an assistant coach, head coach, sports information director, assistant compliance director, summer camp coordinator, and director of on-campus athletic housing. Now, I find myself an athletic administrator. Holding multiple titles and jobs throughout a career is not unique—nor is it particularly unusual that I did this at the NAIA, NCAA Division II, and the Division I levels. Many who have worked in college athletics have *climbed the ladder* and bounced around during their career. What separates my career from most is that I have done it while working for only one institution. From 1985 to 1988, I was employed by *Kennesaw College*; from 1988 to 1996 *Kennesaw State College* was my home; and from 1996 to present I have been a proud employee of *Kennesaw State University*.

I arrived at Kennesaw College in the summer of 1985. I was 23 years old when I was hired to be Kennesaw's first "full-time" assistant women's basketball coach and assistant *slowpitch* softball coach. At that time, the Owls played as members of the NAIA. Its athletic director was the late, great James "Spec" Landrum (*the father of my career*). I owe most of my core coaching philosophies to that dear, sweet, sometimes *bear* of a man. He saw something in me that no one else did (or has since). He gave me my chance.

When I parked my blue 1975 Buick and reported for work on June 1st, I was one of four individuals that would make up what became Kennesaw State University's first core of *full-time* coaches.

Coach Landrum founded Kennesaw College Athletics in 1982. Due to budgetary limits, he employed only *part-time* coaches. It was not until late spring of 1985 that he was able to hire a core of full-time coaches. Even then, the coaches of the soccer, golf, track, and the head softball coach remained part time.

Phil Zenoni and Bret Campbell were paired up in men's basketball. Zenoni, the head basketball coach, also coached the golf team. The basketball assistant Campbell was assigned to also serve as assistant baseball coach. I was given to the head women's basketball coach, Ronda Seagraves to serve as her assistant. In a bit of serendipity, I was also tapped to be the assistant softball coach and to work with (part-time) head coach Medra Ashmore. So, there we were—Kennesaw's first full-time coaches.

I served as Coach Ashmore's assistant for one season. She served, quite successfully, as the slowpitch softball program's head coach for the 1985 season and I joined her for the 1986 campaign, which was as equally successful.

After the 1986 season, for reasons not of her doing, Coach Ashmore left the team and I was named head coach. I was the coach of the Kennesaw College (NAIA) slowpitch softball team from 1987-1990. The team was better than good, they were phenomenal—and I had very little to do with it. When a coach's program can boast a 153-15 five-year record, it is 100 percent because the team had excellent players. That's just a fact.

By the fall of 1988, women's basketball was in my rearview mirror. Softball was my primary responsibility. In addition to my sport, I had a few other responsibilities.

Now, the reason I provided this brief backstory before writing about our 1995 season is that the slowpitch program at Kennesaw College from 1985-1990 is the foundation on which Kennesaw State University's current (fastpitch) softball program was built. When KSC's inaugural fastpitch softball squad took the field for the 1991 regular season, six of its nine starters were playing in the first fastpitch game they had ever seen. Plus, their head coach (*yours truly*) was coaching the sport for the first time. Those six starters were all from slowpitch backgrounds. Their athleticism is why the Owl fastpitch program went from nonexistence in 1990 to being crowned NCAA Division II National Champions in 1995.

The Waples Effect

I cannot write about the 1995 season, or my career, without telling you about David Lloyd Waples. Near the end of the 1986-87 academic year, Coach "Spec" Landrum—Kennesaw State's first athletic director—announced his retirement.

Coach Landrum was who hired me. He had hired all of us. We coaches had a great deal of respect for him and were sad to see him go. He created a great base from which our department grew. He remained a father figure, mentor, and confidant for the rest of his days on Earth. We lost him in 2012. I have yet to fill that void.

By midsummer of 1987, and after a thorough search, Dr. Dave Waples was named Kennesaw College's second athletic director. He had a diverse background. He had been a college instructor, a collegiate coach, and a commissioner of a NCAA Division I Conference (Gulf Star).

If Woody Hayes and Henny Youngman had a kid together it would be Dave Waples. He has both the hellfire and brimstone approach to athletics as did Coach Hayes and he's always equipped with ever ready, somewhat corny jokes such as those of the old standup comic Youngman. To call Dave Waples "a bit quirky" is like calling President Donald Trump "a little polarizing."

Dave is just different. He is lost in the era(s) of 1955-1975, and he ain't changing. That part of his makeup is a doubled-edged sword which has followed him ever since the day we met. He can be a pain in the butt. He is a *Monday morning quarterback*, but he is a *Kennesaw man*.

Coach Waples was an excellent caretaker of university funds—he *hated* to spend a nickel. That being said, in the 23+ years he was my boss, every team I coached always had what was requisite—not only to compete, but to *win*. This was incontrovertible and it was true for all sports within our department over his 23-year tenure.

I have never known anyone who loves to win (and hates to lose) more than the redhead from Grove City, Ohio. Waples is still that way and he is still a pain in the butt after a loss. Today he is enjoying retirement and still failing in his lifelong quest to find a golf swing. He is a friend, an Owl for life, and I will always be grateful to him.

Upon Waples' arrival, there were only a few changes in my world. As part of my new duties assigned by the incoming AD, I was made the department's sports information director and held that post until June of 1995. On the field it was business as usual. Our slowpitch team was still winning everything in sight.

In the late 1980s intercollegiate slowpitch softball was unique to the Southeast. Most of the country was playing fast-pitch, but NAIA District 25 (comprised of schools from Georgia and northern Florida), still played slowpitch. I only mention this because that factor gave our slowpitch team no national tournament in which to compete, thus it limited any potential national acclaim or exposure. This fact bothered Coach Waples from day one.

Early in his tenure Coach Waples made it known that he wanted Kennesaw State to play fastpitch softball. He wanted us to be playing on a national (as opposed to a regional) stage. Knowing his feelings, I knew that day was coming but I was still troubled when Dave asked to meet with me in January of 1989. I knew what was coming. He started the visit by asking a question I did not know was meant to be *rhetorical*. He asked, "What do you think about us being ready to convert to fastpitch by the 1991 regular season?" I quickly replied, "I'm against it. We are dominant in slowpitch. The Georgia high schools play slowpitch and I think it's an awful idea." This is where the *rhetorical* part of his question comes in—he quickly stated, "Well, we are going to do it, and if you want to coach softball here, you'll support the decision." That, my friends, is the day I fell in love with fastpitch softball. I might be hardheaded and opinionated, but I ain't stupid. Plus, I needed a job.

That folks, is how the Kennesaw State College fastpitch softball program was started. After that meeting, all I had to do was: 1.) tell the team—full of good people and athletes—that we were scrapping their program after the 1990 season; 2.) try to at least familiarize myself with fastpitch; 3.) hire an assistant coach who could help me coach a sport about which I knew very little. No problem, right?

To their credit, the 1989 and 1990 teams were as dominant as their four predecessors. We won games and championships and, sadly with very little fanfare, that was that. The most dominant intercollegiate program in the school's history was gone. To this day, I still feel badly for the people that were a part of that era.

Telling the team about what was coming for 1991 was difficult. There were a lot of tears in the room. There were tears for several days. My second task (learning about fastpitch) was a process of traveling, watching, and reading. Ridding myself of onus number three, the hiring of an assistant, was a gift from heaven. Sheer luck and fate put me in the right place, on the right weekend so that I could find Donald James McKinlay—a native of Lethbridge, Alberta, Canada.

Don McKinlay was a senior catcher on Kennesaw State's baseball team in 1989. In '89, in addition to being the head softball coach, I was also the sports information director. In late May, I accompanied the baseball team to Jacksonville, Florida, for their NAIA District 25 Tournament. The '89 softball season was over and it was so much fun to have a week to just watch baseball. As I ran things through my mind as to how was I ever going to get a fastpitch program off of the ground, I became more terrified that I'd fail.

Over the course of the weekend, each time Don came to bat I was impressed with his swing. He attacked the ball effortlessly and he hit it hard. At dinner on the night of the tournament's conclusion, I struck up an informal conversation with Don. I found that he was majoring in education, had another year of school before he would graduate, wanted to coach, and was looking for a job to pay for school.

I quickly started doing the math: the kid has a great swing + he needs a job + I, the head coach of the new sport, cannot hit a lick (and certainly cannot teach it) = *opportunity*.

I did not immediately tip my hand as to what was rattling in my head. Though I was most impressed with his quiet demeanor and as to how he carried himself, I wanted to *take my time* and thoroughly evaluate things. I needed to make certain he was a good fit. Therefore, I gave no indication as to what I was thinking. I played it cool. I offered him the job on the bus ride home.

When evaluating talent, coaches may not always understand what they are seeing, but all good coaches know when they have found something special. Don was, and is, special. I had no idea what we could pay him. I wasn't even completely sure if I could hire him, but I did. As they say, the rest is history. He agreed to come on board starting in the fall of 1989. He would help me coach our final slowpitch season and then we would try to turn the page. It was the best job of talent evaluation and recruiting I ever did.

When together, Donny and I were (and still are) lightening in a bottle. Though we have not worked together since 2003, he can still anticipate my thoughts and ideas better than anyone can. As I have already stated, we meshed right away. Don offset my every weakness. Collectively, we started to develop the plan as to how we could begin the conversion process and not disrupt the 1990 team's season. Looking back, I think that our plan worked out OK. To put it plainly, had there been no Don McKinlay, there would have likely been no Scott Whitlock. He's my brother and I love him.

As we entered the final slowpitch season in 1990, Donny and I knew we would not have enough scholarship money to buy a completely new, experienced fastpitch team for 1991. We were committed to honoring the scholarships of the slowpitch players. So we knew that anyone who could not convert to fastpitch would have to stay *on the payroll* until they cycled out.

Early in the preparations for the '90 season we identified 12-14 slowpitch players who possessed the athleticism that lent itself to the possibility they could be good fastpitch players. As the '90 season rolled along we began to sell them on the idea of trying the new game. Nearly all of them did.

After getting the dozen or so players to buy-in to playing fastpitch (and with losing some players to graduation), we figured we would have enough scholarship money to go find four experienced recruits plus one or two local athletes who we could convert. We set out to go *wherever necessary* in order to find two experienced pitchers, a third baseman, and one experienced catcher. Luckily for us, Dave Waples (even though to hear him tell it, the entire University System of Georgia was *out of money*) gave us the necessary recruiting money to go find them.

For 24 years anytime any coach who went to Waples saying they "needed money," got the same initial response: "You can't do that. We are broke, we don't have any money. Do you know how much money I have already given you this year?" Then the haggling would begin and eventually the coach would almost always get what they *needed* (not *wanted* but *needed*). The discussion would then conclude—usually with the same closing remark. Dr. Waples would always tell the given coach, "THIS IS THE LAST $@^#-ING TIME THAT WE CAN EVER DO THIS. SO, DO NOT ASK FOR ANYTHING EVER AGAIN. AND, THIS TIME, I MEAN IT. DO YOU HEAR ME? I MEAN IT."

And, so it Began

With our strategy and funding limits in hand—and while coaching an outstanding 1990 slowpitch team—Don and I got started. We went about trying to find our four *experienced* fast-pitch players to add to the talent that would join us from our slowpitch roster. The first player we identified was an experienced catcher out of Columbus, Georgia, named Tonya Fowler. She had played one season at Columbus College, but was looking to transfer. She was our first fastpitch recruit. Shoulder problems limited her playing time while with us, but she must have learned something. After graduation, Tonya launched a coaching career that saw her teams make numerous appearances in the state tournament. Her Woodstock High School team won the 5-A (at the time, Georgia's largest high school classification) State Championship in 2006. She is indeed one of my points of pride. Tonya (Fowler) Sebring is retired from coaching and is now the athletic director at the school where she won the state title. I love me some T-Gail.

Me and Tonya (Fowler) Sebring - "T-Gail"

Our second recruit was a junior college (JC) third baseman from Louisburg College, Diane Parham. Man, she could hit. Though she was with us only one season (she later joined the military), she was the anchor to our first infield in 1991.

Kena Wood, another JC player, joined us from Kaskaskia College in Illinois. She was a left-handed pitcher, a native of Mt. Vernon, Illinois, and always had a big smile on her face. She played all of 1991 and most of 1992 in the shadow of the final *experienced* recruit in our small recruiting class, but she earned her place in KSU softball lore in just two days in May of 1992.

All the Way from Calgary, Alberta, Canada

When we found Kena, we felt we had a serviceable pitcher, but she was not dominant. I really wanted our second pitching signee to be the linchpin of our team. We needed someone for whom we could score two runs and then say, *"There you go, finish it."* As much as we tried, we really couldn't find what we wanted. Until...

One morning in the office, while I was whining about not being able to find what I wanted, Don said to me, "Hey Coach, I just remembered that I have a friend back home who has a younger sister who pitches, and she is supposed to be pretty good." When I heard that I thought, *"Great! I am about to start a sport with no pitching depth and Donny wants to get his buddy's little sister a scholarship.*" I responded by saying (paraphrasing), "*We sure have nothing to lose. Have your guy get us a tape of his sis and let's take a look.*"

In two weeks or so, a brown envelope arrived at my office. It was from Calgary, Alberta, Canada—Owls softball had just gone *international*. Inside was a brief letter of introduction and a skills VHS tape of Ms. Dyan Mueller. I watched the tape three or four times before Don arrived. I thought the kid was a pretty good hitter as well as a solid fielder, but her pitching did not *wow* me. After Don watched the tape a few times, he convinced me that, at the time, she might be the best kid available for us. I eventually agreed, but I still was skeptical. That's how we found recruit number four—the one who would prove to be our first star.

After three seasons, 67 wins, 259 strikeouts, a career ERA of 1.01, and a lifetime batting average of .336, I admit that I might have missed on the young lady from Calgary, Canada, during her film evaluation.

Dyan Mueller was the most important recruit the Owl softball program ever signed. We went on to sign *better* players, but, it was upon her shoulders that the entire KSU fastpitch program was built. We could have never gotten out of the block so rapidly had it not been for the drive, talent, leadership, and competitive spirit of the girl we called "Calgary."

She led us to two fourth-place and one national runner-up finishes in our first three years of existence. Again, we have had better players come through our doors in our 26+ years of fastpitch play, but we have never had a more important one. She started it all. That cannot be denied.

The 1990 slowpitch season ended. The team won everything in its sights and played superbly. The day after the season was over, KSC *fastpitch* softball opened for business.

As one would expect, the initial year of fastpitch softball

faced formidable challenges. Our facility, which had been used for slowpitch, had no dugouts, no permanent fence, and only a small section of bleachers for seating. Like baseball, there were no locker rooms or restrooms at the facility. As mentioned previously, only four or five of the players had ever played fastpitch. We knew we had obstacles, but we also knew that we had athletes and fighters. The 13-14 converts to fastpitch saw the task before them as a great challenge. They immersed themselves into it. They welcomed it. Don and I openly admitted to the team that we would all be learning on the fly. We also told them we believed in the people we had assembled. The players got it.

The 1991 team finished 41-11. It produced a 9-0 Tri-District mark including both District and Tri-District Tournament championships. After winning the NAIA Tri-District Championship, we advanced to the national championships where we finished fourth. Mueller was named the Tri-District Player of the Year after going 29-7 with a 0.81 ERA (she also hit .295). Three *slowpitch players*—Leah Crawford, shortstop (.382, 38 RBI), outfielders Kelly McDuffie (.338, 34 RBI) and Cindy Condra (.273)—were named All-District. Not a bad first year.

Recruiting the Freshmen of 1992

The somewhat unexpected success of our program in 1991 allowed us to recruit a better brand of athlete that might not have normally viewed a new program as a desirable possible home. Fastpitch had yet to find its way into the South in 1991. Other than South Carolina and Florida State, no SEC or ACC teams were playing our sport. Therefore, we found that we could make realistic pushes for top tier talent. In addition, Don and I were too young to be scared not to try.

Over the course of the spring and summer of 1991, we signed the most important recruiting class in the program's history. If Dyan Mueller was the most important signing we ever got and Kelly Rafter the most impactful, the five women that were to become the 1995 seniors were and remain the bedrock of Kennesaw State softball. Without Candi Cain, Tonya Carlisle, Tiffany Tanner, Colleen Thorburn, and Wanda Wiggins, who knows if we would have ever built off the success of 1991.

Carlisle and Thorburn were undisputed breakout stars—both multiple time All-Americans—and Colleen also represented Canada in two Olympic Games (1996 & 2000). The character, determination, and class the five of them displayed daily *as a unit* are what set the baseline of what we (coaches and *players*) expected from everyone who wore our jerseys.

During their four years together, the seniors of 1995 led us as the team won 188 of the 211 games played (.891 winning percentage). Tonya Carlisle became the school's first four-time All-American. Colleen Thorburn became an All-American and a two-time Olympian (Canada). Cain, Tanner, and Wiggins were starters for much of the season. When dusk fell on Salem, Virginia, on May 21, 1995, those five seniors were national champions. They had completed the mission and avenged the disappointments of the two previous seasons. They silenced the whispers and answered all questions. I am so glad that I got to see them do it.

The 1992 team almost pulled off the impossible. We fought our way to the championship game of the NAIA World Series, dropping a 3-2 thriller to Pacific Lutheran. Canada native and transfer, outfielder Laura Munson (.487, 57 RBI), was named the Tri-District Player of the Year. Three other KSU players joined her on the All-American team: Kelly McDuffie (.424, 39 RBI), Leah Crawford (.390, 46 RBI), and third baseman Tonya Carlisle (.288). Freshman catcher Colleen Thorburn (.382, 43 RBI), and veteran Dyan Mueller (24-5, 1.05 ERA and .367) were All-Tri-District choices. Mueller, Munson, and Thorburn were Canadian recruits. In the 1990s, *Canadian Owls* were one of the trademarks of our program—in addition to winning.

After Mueller threw two shutout wins (10-0 over Georgian Court and a 6-0 win against Columbia, Missouri) to open the NAIA World Series in Pensacola, Florida, Huntingdon (Alabama) sent the team to the loser's bracket with a 2-0 defeat. During that game while hitting, Mueller had a pitch break her right hand. Senior Kena Wood (17-2, 0.75), who spent the biggest part of her two years as an Owl serving as Muller's understudy, stepped up and brilliantly pitched the Owls past three opponents (allowing only two runs) including a redeeming win over Huntingdon. Wood successfully led KSC into the national finals. In just two days, Kena Wood stepped out of the *great Mueller's shadow* and secured her own place in Owl softball lore. Unfortunately, the magic ended. We were beaten by Pacific Lutheran in the championship finals, but 1992 proved to be a glimpse into the program's future.

Two Years of Disappointment

In 1993, winning streaks of nine, five, three, 14, and four games were sandwiched around four losses as we finished with a 35-4 regular-season mark and the nation's No. 1 ranking. While Milligan (Tennessee) gave us our first-ever District loss, the team went on to race through the Tri-District tournament and make their third-consecutive NAIA World Series appearance.

Two-time All-Americans Tonya Carlisle (.435, 40 RBI), Kelly McDuffie (.411, 31 RBI and the Tri-District Player of the Year), and Laura Munson (.406, 38 RBI) were joined on the All-American team by sophomore (and future two-time Olympian), catcher Colleen Thorburn (.380, 43 RBI) as well as a freshman pitcher who posted a 20-5 record with a 0.77 ERA—Miss Kelly Rafter.

At the national tourney we won a 2-1 opening squeaker over host Columbia (Missouri) and then blasted St. Mary (Texas) 12-1 to enter the winner's bracket semifinal. In the bottom of the fifth with the bases loaded and no one out, trailing Hawaii

Pacific 2-1, the heart of our lineup went down on strikes and the team fell into the loser's bracket. After an 8-1 revenge win over Pacific Lutheran, eventual national champion Oklahoma City ended our season. We finished a disappointing fourth in the nation. Did you hear what I said? We finished a *disappointing* fourth in the nation. That notion in and of itself proves what a double-edged sword *winning* can be.

In 1994 there was more heartache. Again, ranked No. 1 during the entire regular season, we racked up a 48-4 record, a fourth consecutive Tri-District title and another trip to the NAIA World Series. Our regular season losses were to long-time rivals Mobile and Huntingdon. In 1994, we were also going through the transformation from NAIA into NCAA Division II and posted a 16-0 mark against D-II Peach Belt Conference opponents (which would be our new league beginning with the 1995 season).

The 1994 team was a great one. Six players were named NAIA All-Americans: Tonya Carlisle (.348, 45 RBI) was named for the third time; Kelly Rafter (21-1, 0.82) gained her second nod; and Colleen Thorburn (.357, 7 HR, 52 RBI), Tracey Britt (.387, 30 RBI), Nada Hlohovsky (.347), and Jackie Hall (20-3, 0.74) received their first honor.

After coasting through the Tri-District Tournament, we were shocked in game one of the World Series by Grace (Indiana) 2-1. We then plodded through the loser's bracket beating William Woods (Missouri) 3-2, Pacific Lutheran 4-0, Madonna 4-1, and Belmont 9-1 to reach the semifinals. In the semis Athens State dismissed us 6-4. Perhaps the best team that we ever had at KSU left Columbia, Missouri, disappointed yet again. Though we were only a 4-year-old program, to this day many of us associated with those teams feel as if we missed opportunities in 1993 and 1994. As I said earlier, *winning* brings on its own set of perils.

Though we were very proud of what we had accomplished,

after 1994 we immediately started to hear the whispers of, "They just can't win the big one." The fact that a program in only its fourth year of existence (with four top four finishes nationally)—from a state whose high schools did not sponsor the sport they play—was actually being mentioned as "disappointing" was both hurtful and laughable.

What no one but a few of us knew was that the Class of 1995 was still hungry and (luckily for all of us) they were *not happy*.

The Story of 1995

As we began our preparation for the 1995 season (in September of '94), most of us had a bitter taste in our mouths. Don and I were dissatisfied—plus 11 of the 18 on the roster who had played on the 1994 team were angry. As a result, we had the proverbial *chip on our shoulder* and it remained there until late May of 1995.

As I eluded to, over the course of the summer of 1994: Even though we were *only a 4-year-old program* and *had finished in the top four* in each of our *first four seasons* of existence—coaches and players were hearing whispers and answering questions about *not being able to win the big one.* By fall of 1994 we were tightly strung and ready to take people's heads off. We did not care that we were moving from NAIA to D-II. We didn't give a damn about a new division or a different conference. We knew we had a good, experienced team and we wanted to shut everybody up.

The fall went very smoothly. I griped, Don soothed, and the gals got better every day—business as usual. Seven of our nine starters were returnees. We had rookies at shortstop and in center field, but there were veterans all over the place. Our fall was all about getting ourselves ready to go. When we broke for winter we felt really good about our club.

When we returned in January it went pretty much like the previous four. We conditioned, trained, and prepared. So when opening day rolled around on Valentine's Day, we jumped all over our first opponent within our new level of competition by sweeping West Georgia 9-0 and 26-1 in a doubleheader. We took a *step up* for four games by traveling to Division I's Furman and Georgia Southern, splitting a pair of doubleheaders. As February ended and after six games, we were sitting at 4-2 and felt OK about things.

March 3 and 4, 1995

Our first regular-season tournament of 1995 was held in Carrollton (hosted by West Georgia) on March 3rd and 4th. It was to be a four-game, guarantee tourney with single-elimination bracket play at the end.

The two days of practice prior to going to Carrollton were sluggish. We coaches didn't think too much about it because the week was a bit chilly. On the opening day of play (a Friday) it went from chilly to very cold. We had two games on day one. Early afternoon we won easily. In the nightcap we played sloppy as Jacksonville State edged us 5-4 on a very frigid night. At night's end we had a team meeting, I (likely) made a mountain out of a molehill and sternly challenged the team and told them that their quality of play was unacceptable. I really gave it to them.

On day two the weather turned from cool to windy and bitterly frigid. The entire time the sun was up on Saturday, March 4, 1995, the temperature never got above 35 and we played in a 20+ mph wind. In the day's opening game the team took my Friday night's speech out on Lincoln Memorial 11-0. We then beat (*what is now*) West Alabama.

Those two wins gained us the second seed in the four-team, championship bracket. In the semis we quickly dismissed Tusculum 5-0. It was after 7 p.m. at game's end. The temperature had fallen into the low 20s and the wind was still steady as well as crisp. I was so cold at the end of the Tusculum game that I could not stop my teeth from chattering. I was frozen to my core. I was in such a bad way that I convinced my dear friend—the late Tom Sirmon—to give me the second pair of sweats he was wearing atop his first. I made my case by telling him that he could go watch the finals from the bus, but I had to be out in that crap. Therefore, I needed his pants. Luckily for me, he obliged. Tommy Sirmon was a sweet man. The last decade of his life was full of sickness and pain. I was sad for us, but happy for him when he went to be with the Lord in 2016. Miss ya' Tommy.

When we took the field for the finals against Columbus State, a conference foe, it was after 9 p.m. The arctic air was brutal. No one wanted to be there and we lost 2-0. We went 4-2 on the weekend of March 3-4 in 1995. As we drove back to Kennesaw, trying to get warm and regain feeling in our hands and feet, we were an 8-4 team. The season prior, we lost only four games all year. We were asking ourselves, "Is Division II that big of a jump?" "What are we doing wrong?" We knew that we had to get better before we really start questioning ourselves.

In my head I could already hear the "win the big one" questions being replaced with the, "I knew that they'd struggle playing in Division II." The latter question had merit. We did struggle—for about *three days*. After the 2-0 loss to Columbus on that frosty night in Carrollton on March 5th, the next time the Owls would meet to discuss a loss it would be May 18th— 40-consecutive wins later.

The Start of a Roll

A coach should never underestimate the pride that lives in champions. I should have not worried about being 8-4 out of the gate. I was coaching a senior-heavy, talented softball team. I should have known that they would fix things. Boy did they ever.

Naturally, I like to report that I made some big adjustment to our lineup or made a profound speech that turned us around, but honesty compels me to say I have no tangible reason as to *why* what happened next occurred. No one will likely know what happened on March 5-7. All I know is that between us leaving Carrollton frozen and the next game on the following Wednesday, the Kennesaw State Owls softball team GOT HOT!

When our school made the move from NAIA to NCAA Division II, we joined the Peach Belt Athletic Conference. In 1995 it was a league made up of schools in Georgia and the Carolinas. We had played a PBAC schedule in 1994 (going 16-0), but due to our transition from NAIA to D-II we were not eligible to compete in their conference tournament. 1995, however, was a different story.

When we opened our first NCAA D-II conference schedule play on Wednesday, March 8, our team did not know it was starting a journey that was to be historic. We easily handled Augusta in a twin bill. The next day we went down to Milledgeville and blanked Georgia College twice. At week's end we had a meek four-game winning streak. We were 12-4 and 4-0 in our new conference. More importantly, we had regained our mojo. We were again walking around the ballpark *looking the part* and we were again a confident bunch. Now it wasn't all hugs and smiles. As always, I could still (unintentionally) find a way to get the players mad or stirred up about something. Or, two of the players could get mad with one another, but we all knew that we were gaining on *it*.

After Georgia College, it was eight days before we were to play again in Greenwood, South Carolina, against Lander. I was worried about losing our momentum or edge, but my fears were unwarranted. We reeled off six more PBAC wins before edging Delta State and sweeping North Alabama. On March 26th and 29th we notched four more conference wins at the expense of SC-Spartanburg and Georgia College. So after all the angst, back when our teeth were chattering 25 days earlier on that Saturday night in Carrollton, the '95 Owls were alive and well at the midpoint of their first year of NCAA D-II play. We were 25-4 overall and 10-0 in the PBAC and we were in the midst 17-game winning streak.

Carlisle and Thorburn were doing what seniors do. They were driving in and scoring runs. An emerging sophomore Cara Dornstauder aided them. She too was hitting everything in sight. We had so many playing well, but if I had to point a finger at why we were gaining so much steam, I would have to point at our quirky, unexplainable junior pitcher who in our first 29 games had established herself as a true star and a work-horse. I am talking about Miss Kelly Rafter.

I have met a lot of characters in my life. I know people from just about every continent on our planet, but I have never known anyone like Kelly Louise Rafter.

I saw Kelly Rafter pitch for the first time in Valdosta, Georgia, during the fall of 1991. She was playing travel ball for one of metro-Atlanta's few 18-under fastpitch teams—the Lilburn T-Birds. The T-Birds were playing in an exhibition tournament in early October. As I walked up on their 10 a.m. game I noticed this huge flock of hair that had a great pitching arm under it. Back then Kelly's hairdo made her look like the lead singer in the *Bangles* on their "Walk Like an Egyptian" video. Lots of hair.

It was obvious the kid had *presence* and command of her pitches, including a changeup (an off-speed pitch that could make hitters look downright silly). I was extremely happy when we were able to coax her into joining our team in the fall of 1992. I knew that we had signed a good one, but I had no idea that we had signed the best pitcher to ever wear an Owls jersey.

As I mentioned previously, Kelly was a little different. While Candi Cain or Paige Wofford read books during bus rides, Kelly colored them. She would con her mom into driving 45 miles (one way) to do her laundry. Kelly is a very intelligent woman, but attending class was an "inconvenience" that she tolerated so she could play ball. When I'd ask Kelly about her academic progress, I'd always get the same short update: "I'm eligible Coach." Off the field, she was really something.

On the field, she was special, very special. She had parted with the wild hair prior to arriving onto our campus, but she did bring that right arm—that magical right arm (and that right arm brought its changeup). In 1993 she joined the "Great Mueller" in the rotation and won a team high 20 games. In 1994 she asserted herself firmly as the Owls' ace winning 21.

In 1995, BOOM! Kelly Rafter was named Division II's Player of the Year after going 32-5 with a 0.85 ERA. A legend was born and it hovers over Bailey Park to this day. In 1996 Kelly completed her career by posting 31 more victories.

When it was all over Kelly Rafter was a four-time All-American and compiled a career record of 104-14 with an ERA of 0.82. She carried the 1995 and 1996 Owls to back-to-back national championships. Simply put, she was the best I ever coached.

Our Coming Out Party

The weekend of March 31st-April 2nd we carried that 17-game streak and the momentum to Owensboro, Kentucky, for a midseason tournament. It was going to be our first real D-II challenge. For the first time, the 1995 Owls were going to face several nationally-ranked teams in the same weekend. As I recall, I was both eager and nervous about the opportunity. It was going to be eight games over three days (unheard of today) and we were scheduled to open with a top-five team—Pittsburg State. In the game we quickly fell behind 2-0, but after a five-run third we cruised to a 9-2 win. In the second game, we squeaked by host Kentucky Wesleyan 6-4.

Day two started by defeating another ranked school, Southern Indiana, 7-0. Nationally-ranked Wayne State (Michigan) was next on Saturday. We got by them 5-4. We had several hours off before we played the day's third game. I remember us talking about how we now knew that "we belonged."

Saturday's nightcap became legendary among those present. We played the powerful Wisconsin-Parkside for the first time. On a cold night we outlasted them 6-5. That game was full of unique events. All there witnessed our freshman center fielder, Shannon McDonough, run down a 300-foot fly ball (the complex at which we were playing had no fastpitch fences). That night we saw a laser shot of a line drive ricochet off our pitcher's (Brenda Farrell) leg and come into our dugout. It was in that game I met one of my closest friends—the then-head coach of Parkside, Tory Acheson. More about Wisconsin-Parkside later.

On Sunday, the tournament's final day, we still had three tough games back-to-back-to-back. From the outset, Don and I were concerned—Saturday was very emotional for us. We scored three big wins, won five games total in this meat grinder of a tournament, and were tired.

To their credit, Tonya Carlisle and the rest of the seniors got the team up enough so that we could navigate the day and win three more. We blanked Valdosta State and Carson Newman (4-0; 2-0) before we downed Mississippi College for Women 7-3 to end the trip.

We were a happy bunch when we left Owensboro. We'd won eight tough games (in three days) and stretched our winning streak to 25. More importantly, we left Kentucky knowing that we could play with anybody within Division II. Everyone in Division II now knew that the little ole team from Kennesaw, Georgia, was for real. We felt like championship material, but the lessons learned in our recent two seasons reminded us there was still a long way to go.

* * *

Two paragraphs ago I mentioned Tonya Carlisle. She was a hell of a player. She won all the awards, she's in the KSU Hall of Fame, and she was one of my favorite players with which I worked.

I found Tonya Carlisle (T.C.) kind of by accident during the spring and early summer of 1991. Future Owl, Wanda Wiggins, was pitching for a fastpitch Little League team out of Columbus, Georgia. The team was coached by Mike Bruce. (He is a good man, who during his coaching days tried to help as many kids as he could.) Coach Bruce was well aware of our interest in Wiggins. She was a lefty pitcher/first baseman and we wanted her. Mike Bruce had the best team in the Columbus area and his team advanced within Little League play and was headed to a regional tourney in Charlotte, Tennessee. I called Mike to let him know I'd be coming to the regional. Yes, I went to Charlotte, *Tennessee*. That's not an error—college coaches will go wherever necessary to see/find good players. Anyway...

When I called Mike to let him know I was coming to Charlotte, he informed me that he had recently added a kid who plays third base. He told me that her name was Tonya Carlisle and that she had played with one of the other Columbus teams. He went on to tell me that she had a chance to be a good college player. He was right. Not only did Tonya grow into a good college player, she became a Kennesaw State softball legend and the school's first four-time All-American. Today she is a fine high school coach, a great mom, and my baby sister.

T.C.'s and my relationship is fire tested and real. When she came to Kennesaw State she came with a great competitive spirit, a big heart, and she was a fighter. She had to be. She, her mom, and brother were still learning to live without her late father (who I never met). T.C. was homesick at times and worried a lot about her mom.

As with many of my players, I coached with a style different from anyone for whom T.C. had played. The vast majority of my career, I worked with an *in-your-face* demeanor while on the field. I was rigid and blunt—sometimes too blunt. Trust me, I am not bragging, but in 1991 it was the only style I knew. The older you get, the better your rearview mirror gets. I eventually mellowed as a coach but was never a *walk in the park*. On the flip side, in our program's early years I felt we had to make up for any lack of experience by being tougher and more willing than our opponents. I also wanted our players to develop character, know about accountability, and to be able to handle any tough spot life might throw them. Again, I am not bragging about my coaching style, I am just trying to (right, wrong, or in between) explain what my thinking was back then.

At first T.C. did not respond well to my approach. I scared her to death, but my *pushing her past her daily limits* on occasion is where our relationship and trust was (and remains) anchored. I knew quickly that she could be a good one. I knew we needed her to start as a rookie and I knew she was struggling with issues *back home* among other stuff. I felt those burdens were weighing her down a bit. Therefore, I created a distraction—me. I would get her extremely mad at me so that for at least two and a half hours a day, she'd forget about her problems and only concern herself with shutting me up. I suppose it worked to some extent because she began to play and play well. I pushed T.C. and showed so much attention to her that some of her teammates started thinking of her as the coach's pet (though it was unintended, they might have been a bit right).

T.C. - Hanging on my every word (Ha!)

T.C. slowly began to trust me. She realized that I believed in her and I continued to push her. One of the best indications that our relationship was growing strong happened on the day that T.C.—in the middle of one of my rants—informed me she'd "had enough" in front of the entire team. At that point neither of us knew what to say or do. I think it scared us both a bit. In an instant and as a freshman, Tonya Carlisle gained the respect of the entire team (and her coach). That day she taught me how to be both a better coach and person. It was also the moment that I *knew* she was something special.

T.C.'s career numbers speak for themselves. She was a captain of our 1995 team, and an assistant coach for our 1996 National Championship team. From 1992 'til this day she is a part of my social conscience and always shoots me straight. I love and respect Tonya Carlisle.

* * *

Finishing the Regular Season

We left Owensboro on a 25-game winning streak and with all of Division II aware of who we were. After arriving home we resumed our work. I do not recall if our winning streak was ever openly talked about. A 25-game streak can get heavy, but our players did not let it. They just kept doing their thing. Kelly Rafter and Dee Webb handled the mound and the others kept coming up with clutch hits.

We clicked off nine straight to finish the regular season and swept through the Peach Belt Conference Tournament in three —beating Columbus 5-4 in the finals. Winning the league tournament assured us a berth in the D-II regionals. The regular season and conference tournament were over, and we were 45-4 (winners of 37 in a row). Not bad for a team in its first year of competing at a new level (NCAA D-II).

A Tough Decision

You would think that any coach who is riding 37-straight wins would never *mess with the streak.* You would think. Due to our conference's schedule and other factors, we had a 19-day gap between the end of the Peach Belt Tournament and game one of the NCAA Regionals. Therefore, we (Don and I) went to work trying to tweak the team for the playoffs.

After our conference tourney we were unsatisfied with our team's consistency. We felt we needed to be much sharper in the playoffs. For all of 1995 we really did not have a true leadoff hitter and our strong pitching had shaded defensive weaknesses. We knew the opposition would only get tougher if we progressed. We committed ourselves to the notion that *we are what we are offensively, so let's commit to putting our best defensive team on the field in every inning.* Looking back, I guess sometimes you just get lucky. We made a good decision.

After exploring every option, we made the decision to bring junior Nada Hlohovsky in from left field to play second base, insert senior Tiffany Tanner in left, and sit our *senior* second baseman Candi Cain. Installing the moves were the second-hardest things I ever faced as a head coach. Having to tell Candi of our plans was clearly the hardest.

Candi Cain was our starting second baseman for 35 games in 1995. She was, and remains, a wonderful person. A hard worker and a hustler who never got into trouble. She was a fantastic student and great teammate. Candi, in our opinion, was fading a bit as the season ended.

Once we made everyone aware of the moves, Candi Cain showed the world her true character. A lesser person might have quit and walked away, but not Candi. Each day she continued to come to the ballpark and work hard. She continued to be the consummate teammate and supported her head coach. I still use her attitude throughout that ordeal as an example to this day. When we won the national championship in 1995 Candi was as happy as anyone. *Class act.*

As much as it killed me to give Candi the news, I was convinced those moves would give us our best chance of success during our postseason push. We felt that the position swaps would give us more speed in the outfield and a consistent infield. That was the bottom line.

Regionals

The four-team South Regional was played in Columbus, Georgia. The field was comprised of Carson Newman (winners of the South Atlantic Conference), at-large berthed Columbus (runners-up to us in the PBAC), Florida Southern (champions of the Sunshine State Conference and 1993's national champions), and Kennesaw State.

Two of our three opponents were familiar to us. We faced Carson-Newman several times back in the NAIA days (and once in the season). Of course we were very much aware of Columbus. Both teams were well coached and formidable. Florida Southern was new for us. They were the favorites to advance from Columbus. Just like the teams we faced in Owensboro, we knew playing Florida Southern would a great test.

The seedings saw us open the regional against Columbus. As it was in our two previous meetings in 1995, the game was emotional and tight. We won 3-1. Carson-Newman won their opener against Florida Southern. As a result, we squared off in the winner's side of the draw. Kelly Rafter was dominant, and we advanced with a 1-0 win. Then we sat and waited while the loser's bracket unfolded. Florida Southern eliminated Columbus and avenged their loss to Carson-Newman. That set up Florida Southern versus Kennesaw State.

In preparing our club for the final day, Don and I felt that we had several things in our favor:

1. With the tourney's format being double elimination, Florida Southern would have to beat us twice in order to advance.
2. They were coming off two emotional wins.
3. We were well rested.
4. Most importantly, we had Kelly Rafter on the mound.
5. We were coaching an experienced, confident, and *hungry* team.

Our hunch was validated in one game. Rafter was outstanding, our defense was spot on, and our offense provided us three runs with which to work. We closed the deal 3-0 and walked off the field with a 48-4 record and 40-game winning streak. In our first year playing within the NCAA, Kennesaw State's softball team was on its way to Salem, Virginia, to compete in the 1995 Division II World Series.

The World Series

As we headed to the World Series we were both confident and anxious. We knew we had a good club and had *been there before*, but we also knew that we were playing in a new division. We could not wait to play.

The tournament's draw saw us pitted against Wisconsin-Parkside out of the Central Regional. We had played them earlier in the year in Owensboro. We knew how good they were. It was an exciting game. They hit a home run late in the game to beat us 4-3.

The 40-game streak was gone and for the third-straight year we found ourselves in the World Series' loser's bracket after just one game. It would have been easy for us to take the bait and feel sorry for ourselves. After having to deal with our past disappointments, we knew that someone out there was saying, "Here we go again. They got there, but just can't seem to close the deal." Though the team was disappointed, it only took our players about 10 minutes to hit their reset button.

They collectively picked themselves up and asked, "When do we play tomorrow?" The feelings were nothing like those of 1993 or 1994—they seemed to know how to handle the moment. Perhaps we had learned from the past because we were confident and totally in control of ourselves. Before we left the field that night we openly discussed that nothing had occurred that could not be easily corrected by *a little ole five-game winning streak.*

Our Little Ole Five-Game Winning Streak

Our **second game** of the tournament (or should I say *the first of the five)* matched us against the defending national champions Merrimack (Massachusetts). Kelly Rafter pitched well, and Cara Dornstauder drove in two in the bottom of the seventh as we beat them 4-3.

In our **third game** of the tournament, *the second of the five,* an opportunity for *revenge* was placed clearly in view when Bloomsburg (Pennsylvania) sent Parkside to the bottom half of the bracket in the tournament's fourth game. In the rematch we got our money's worth. Rafter was on and seven of our nine hitters drove in at least one run as we defeated the No. 1-ranked team 9-1. Postgame, we were happy, but nowhere near satisfied.

We celebrated the Parkside win for only about 10 minutes because in our next outing we had to face a powerful

Humboldt State (California) team in the finals of the loser's bracket—with only 30 minutes to prepare.

Our **fourth game** of the tournament, *the third of the five*, was going to be the toughest challenge we faced all season. The team from Northern California was loaded. Earlier in the day they lost 2-1 to Bloomsburg in the winner's bracket final (and they were not in a good mood). They had perhaps the tournament's best player in shortstop, Apple Gomez.

Going into the game we felt good. We were playing solid defense and we were hitting the ball. Our lone concern was that Kelly Rafter had just finished pitching six innings and was up to 20 over the last three days. We did not know what she had left in the tank, but there was no debate in our dugout she was pitching that game.

The Humboldt game was scoreless for the first four and a half innings until they scored two in the bottom of the fifth. We answered with a pair of our own in the sixth. Rafter lowered her cap and held them scoreless in their sixth. In the top of the seventh we got to their reliever Kelly Wolfe and scored two. After that, it was all Rafter. We advanced 4-2.

After losing our opening game of the tournament, 48 hours later we found ourselves on a three-game winning streak and headed into the NCAA Division II World Series Championship round. We were set to face Bloomsburg—a great team, with a fabulous pitcher (April Paoli) and led by a Hall of Fame coach (Jan Hutchinson). We knew how good they were. We knew to win the championship we would have to beat them twice, but we also knew that we were good, too.

Bloomsburg

The morning of May 21, 1995, was quiet at the hotel. As I recall the championship game was set for noon. As we made our way to Moyer Park things were normal. The players were excited, Don was calm, and I was trying not to throw up. Our game plan was simple: give the ball to Kelly Rafter, score her a few runs, and force a *winner take all* second game. We did just that.

Our **fifth game** of the tournament, *the fourth of the five*, featured two of the best pitchers the country had to offer in 1995. Bloomsburg's April Paoli was an All-American. She was legit. She and her teammates had won a very strong Mid-Atlantic Regional. Her numbers spoke for themselves. With her team winning throughout the early rounds of the World Series, she only had to throw two games in the double-elimination tournament. In beating Wisconsin-Parkside and Humboldt State, she only gave up one run in 14 innings of work. She was impressive, but we had a plan.

We had a pitcher to face Miss Paoli named Kelly Rafter. Perhaps I have already mentioned her? An All-American in her own right, Rafter had become the talk of the tournament having pitched 27 innings over three days. "How long can she go?" "What does she have left?" We heard all the questions that morning. Her three wins had not been as flashy as Paoli's, but they had been gutty—and in championship play, guts will beat flash nearly every time. Rafter had been amazing in the tournament, but she saved her best for the last day.

In the 12 p.m. game on May 21, 1995, Kelly Rafter allowed only three hits and even had an RBI as we blanked the Huskies. She was dominant and outperformed April Paoli. Our defense played clean. We followed the game plan and scored two runs in the fourth and one in the seventh. Rafter never gave them a chance. We won by a final score of 3-0.

It was all set. At 3 p.m. on May 21, 1995, an "if necessary" game would be played to decide the NCAA Division II National Champion. Bloomsburg and Kennesaw State. Paoli (21 innings) and Rafter (34 innings)—winner take all.

The Championship Game

Our **sixth game** of the tournament, *the fifth of the five*, was a great college softball game. The first five innings saw the pitching dominate and the sixth started with a 0-0 score.

In the top of the sixth Colleen Thorburn drove in Shannon McDonough who had singled and been sacrificed to second by Nada Hlohovsky. Tonya Carlisle's single plated Thorburn with the inning's second run. When our half-inning concluded we were up 2-0 and six outs from a national championship. As mentioned, Thorburn drove in one run and scored another in the top of the sixth. She really came through for us—*and she was not done.* She was quite a player.

* * *

How many NAIA softball coaches have the father of a two-time Olympian call them on the phone wanting to know more about their 1-year-old program? It happened to me.

There is no way that I could tell the story of the 1995 season —or KSU softball history for that matter—without talking about Colleen Thorburn. She is one of the two or three best players to wear a KSU softball uniform. She was a catcher who could hit the ball out of the park or beat out a bunt for a single and she could most certainly score from first on a double.

One day in the spring of 1991 I received a phone call from Mr. Leon Thorburn. He started our talk by telling me that his work was calling for him and his family to relocate to the Atlanta area from Toronto, Ontario. After only a minimal amount of small talk, Leon was and remains a straight to the point person. He asked me to tell him about our school and our softball team. Without knowing exactly where the conversation was headed I did as he asked. When I paused he told me that he had a daughter that was a good player. I thought to myself, "Oh yeah, what dad doesn't?" Recruiting 101: Every daddy has a daughter that is a "good player." He then mentioned that she had been identified as one of Canada's top junior players. My ears perked up a bit. He then told me that she was a catcher. The man then had my full attention. I quickly suggested that we exchange all needed contact information and that we get his family over for a campus visit as soon as possible. He agreed. That call was perhaps the most important call that I ever received from a player's parent.

When the dust settled with the recruiting, we signed Colleen Thorburn. Her blind faith in what we were trying to do and her trusting us to be worthy of coaching someone with her credentials and talents legitimized us as a softball program. When her career ended she—along with the other freshmen of 1992—had notified the softball world (or, at least our little corner of it) that KSU was serious about its new program and that we were built to last.

Colleen amassed nearly every accolade one can during her career. She was a two-time All-American, she had a career batting average of .381 (never had a season below .357), she still holds the school records for runs scored (199) and triples (47), and her name can be found in no less than eight top 10 career offensive categories. She was also the primary catcher for Owl pitching stars Dyan Mueller and Kelly Rafter.

After her collegiate career ended Colleen represented Canada in the 1996 and 2000 Olympic Games. It was amazing to see her play representing her native country. Today she, her husband Lane, and children reside in the Kennesaw area.

* * *

Oh yeah, back to the game. When we went onto the field to play defense in the bottom of the sixth, we knew that we had a two-run lead, had Kelly Rafter on the mound, that Bloomsburg was a great team, and it was unlikely that they would go quietly. They didn't.

The Huskies grabbed a run back in their half of the sixth,

and we led 2-1 going into the final inning (or so we thought), but Bloomsburg had grabbed a little piece of momentum with their run.

April Paoli had pitched great for 13 innings that day. She had shaken off the disappointment of losing the day's first game and had pitched her tail off and given her team an opportunity to win the second. The run in the bottom of the sixth seemed to give her a boost because in the top of the seventh she handled our 6-7-8 hitters with ease. We headed back out on to the field to play defense—three outs away from the championship.

In the bottom of the seventh, for the first time all week, Kelly Rafter looked a bit tired. She had pitched more than 40 innings in four days and fatigue showed a bit. After an out, a walk, and a hit had tied the game, the Bloomsburg side of the field exploded. Momentum walked directly to and sat in their dugout. Kelly got us out of it, but when she came to the dugout you could see she was tired. We headed to extra innings in the national championship game with no momentum and an exhausted pitcher.

They say that the best measure of a team's character is the way they respond to adversity. I believe that. The eighth inning of game two in Salem, Virginia, at Moyer Park on May 21, 1995, affirmed my belief. Paoli was seemingly in complete control. She retired Shannon McDonough and Nada Hlohovsky for two quick outs and the Husky dugout was rocking. Then Colleen Thorburn came to the plate with two out and no one on. During her at-bat she fought off a great pitch from Paoli and sent a slow roller out toward shortstop. Being a superior athlete, our catcher had no problem beating out an infield single on a ball that traveled maybe 50 feet. So, with two out and a runner with good speed on first, our DH, Cara Dornstauder of Calgary, Alberta, came to the plate. *She was 0-for-6 on the day versus April Paoli.*

* * *

Canada has been good to the Kennesaw State softball program. Dyan Mueller, Colleen Thorburn, Laura Munson, Nada Hlohovsky, Brenda Farrell, Julie Eggert, Kathy Le, Jeri DeWulf, Nikki Scholer, Tara Hrycuik, Cambria McKay, and Jennifer Hunt are just some of the great Canadian players that have worn our brand. There is one on which I wish to expand.

Though all of those mentioned in the previous paragraph are special to me, the best clutch hitter our program has ever had was a shortstop turned designated hitter, turned first baseman from Calgary, Alberta. Her name is Cara Dornstauder. Cara was a great hitter. She has a keen sense of humor and could swing it when money was on the table.

Don McKinlay being a native of Lethbridge, Alberta, had provided us an inside track in landing our first great pitcher, Dyan Mueller. That, in addition to us being lucky enough to have Colleen Thorburn land on our doorstep, really opened the door for us up north. Somehow along the way, we were introduced to a youth coach in Calgary by the name of Geri Dornstauder. We were told she had a daughter with a great eye and good hands. Her name was Cara. When we got to see her play, Cara was better than advertised. I mean she could really swing it. Eventually, we were fortunate enough to convince her to come to Georgia and the rest is history. History that she made.

As you will soon read, Cara played a huge role in our success of 1995. She also hit a three-run jack to put the 1996 national championship on ice for the Owls. I had the privilege of coaching scores of fine softball players, but no hitter had a better knack of coming through in the clutch than Cara Dornstauder.

After a legendary career, graduating, and becoming an educator, Cara married an All-American slugging catcher from

KSU's baseball program, Ryan Coe. Today Ryan, Cara, and their family live in the Kennesaw area. Although he played professionally with the Houston Astros organization, Ryan will always be the second-best hitter in his family—of that there is no doubt.

* * *

As I said, with two out and a runner with good speed on first, our DH, Cara Dornstauder, came to the plate (*0-for-6 on the day versus Paoli*). Big-time players show up at big moments. Cara showed up. BANG! She drove a ball deep to the center field wall. With there being two outs, Thorburn was moving and there was no way I was about to hold her at third. In an instant, momentum showed its fickleness and sprinted to our dugout as Colleen Thorburn slide in safe at home. Suddenly we were up 3-2 and again three outs from a national championship. After being silent all day, Cara stood atop second base. She looked at me and all she did was remind me that she knew there were two outs.

Now here I must confess, after Cara's double and Tonya Carlisle making the final out in our eighth, I honestly cannot remember hearing a sound for the next four to six minutes. That's all it took for Rafter to finish it. Despite having already pitched 41 innings that week, the look on Kelly Rafter's face told us that it was over as she went out to pitch the eighth. What happened was surreal. It only took four pitches.

The inning's first pitch was a changeup. It got us a ground ball to third—Carlisle to Wiggins. One out. After a curve ball missed, a changeup induced a soft pop fly (in foul territory) to Wiggins at first. Two outs. Then a first pitch changeup changed our lives. It got us another big hopper to Carlisle at third—*she ran it half way over*—before tossing it over to Wiggins to end the game.

Kelly Rafter had finished making her statement by saying, "Enough is enough!" She had sensed that everyone's nerves—including her head coach's—had been stressed to their limits and she used only four pitches, *three of which were changeups*, to finish it and to seal the national championship.

* * *

Dogpile celebration after winning the '95 World Series

After Wiggins caught the ball, I recall seeing the players begin to storm toward the mound from all directions. My next memory is of me in front of the dugout on all fours pounding the ground with my right fist and, as always, Don waiting there for me. That was the first moment I finally began hearing sound again since the middle of the eighth inning. That is no exaggeration.

After I got up, Don gave me a huge hug. We then joined the celebration on the mound. I think I hugged everyone—fans, parents, my family, the field crew, and of course the players. Never let it be said that a person cannot feel joy, relief, and validation at the exact same time. One can, in fact, experience such emotions simultaneously.

* * *

What a relief: Don and I show off the championship trophy

The championship ceremony is a bit of blur for me. We had seven players named to the All-Tournament Team, led by Kelly Rafter:

- Kelly Rafter: 42 IP, 5 wins, 30 K's, 8 BB
- Cara Dorndstauder: 8 for 18 (.444), 7 RBI, 4 doubles
- Colleen Thorburn: 11 for 22 (.500), 7 RBI, 7 runs
- Nada Hlohovsky: 9 for 23 (.391), 6 runs
- Tonya Carlisle: 5 for 18 (.277), 6 PO, 20 assists
- Shannon McDonough: 4 for 17 (.235), 2 RBI, 3 runs
- *Paige Wofford: Zero at bats, *Defensive Wizardry*

Folks, Paige Wofford's tournament is no misprint. Pitcher Kelly Rafter hit for herself, therefore, right fielder Paige Wofford never hit in the tournament. However, over the four days she thrilled the crowd with her defensive skills. It was an amazing (no overstatement) performance.

After the ceremony, there were pictures taken and more hugs. Oh, were there hugs! After we finished at Moyer Park we headed for the vans, but before heading to the hotel, we had one stop to make.

Let's All Go Down to the River

Moyer Park is partially abutted to the Roanoke River. At some point of the week we decided that if we won the championship we would all go jump in the river. We did. Everybody splashed and played like kids. We were a tired but happy group. Someone found an old broom on one of its banks and there are photos of different ones of us holding up the broom as if to say, *"We have just swept up five games, a national championship, and we're damn proud."* I will never forget that.

Other Memories of that Night

- I had to call the game results and story into the *Marietta Daily Journal.* At the time I still had the dual responsibility of being Kennesaw State's Sports Information Director (SID).

- I placed a call to Dr. Waples to give him the news. He was in a meeting and was unavailable to take my call so I left this message, "Tell him to order the rings and that his SID just quit."

- I called my Granny to tell her that her baby was a national champion. She responded to the news by asking, "Did you win all of your games?" I replied, "NO, but we won the championship." She followed that with, "Who beat you?" UGH. I loved my Granny, she is one of God's saints, but she had no appreciation for that moment. I guess it was because in her eyes her grandkids were champions every day.

- My clearest post-river memory of May 21, 1995, was that I could not sleep that night, but I laid there so relieved. Yes, *relief* is the word that best described how I felt after the initial rush faded away. I was relieved that I would never have to answer anyone's stupid questions or listen to some faux lamentation for our not winning the championship. Our young softball program had just completed its fifth consecutive World Series appearance and the best I could muster was a sense of relief. I guess that kind of sums up the life of a coach: *"Winning only brings temporary relief for coaches because we all know we have that next game coming up."* You may quote me.

'95 National Champion KSU Owls Softball Team

The season of 1995 changed not only my life, it changed many lives. I will always be grateful to Don McKinlay and especially the players for letting me tag along.

20

THE DAY BILLY GRAHAM DIED

I had been looking forward to Wednesday, February 21, 2018, for some time. Later that afternoon I was to go on a trip. I was invited by a friend to be a part of a group of four that would travel to southern Florida for three days of deep-sea fishing—*kite fishing* to be exact. We were going after big ones. Whereas I have fished in lakes, ponds, rivers, and creeks my entire life, I had very limited time on salt water, so this should've been a great adventure.

I spent the previous night overpacking. The boat's cabin rooms would allow us to sleep on board—*just like the Kennedys*. Never having this privilege, I really didn't know how to pack. Therefore, I had a little bit of everything in my bag.

Shortly after arriving at my office on the morning of my departure for fishing, I learned the Reverend Billy Graham had relocated to his heavenly home. I cried a bit. As a Christian, I was filled with a sense of great loss and vacancy within my soul. I never met him. I only saw him preach once in person, but Rev. Graham was (at least to me) God's *main man on Earth*. With all due reverence and respect to His Holiness the Pope (and all my

Catholic brethren), I am a Protestant and Billy Graham was my spiritual beacon. I know that many others feel the same way.

As I sat at my computer, reading the stories and tributes, I was reminded of how Billy Graham was able to simplify and share the most complex choice that we humans face. Heaven or Hell? Billy Graham made God accessible to any who would listen. He gave hope to the hopeless. Millions upon millions of people—of all nationalities, races, and economic lots—were told that in God's eyes all are important. More importantly, he preached that each of us are eligible for pardon. I found great comfort in that.

While I was reflecting on all this, someone came by my office to wish me luck on the fishing trip. That brief greeting threw me straight back to Billy Graham. Now, there was a real angler. Here I am, fired up about trying to catch marlins, sunfish, and other *big fish*, but for over seven decades, Billy Graham went after the most elusive and gnarly fishes of them all—human souls. Perhaps not since Saint Paul has an individual worked so hard to let people worldwide know that there is hope, as did Billy Graham. I will miss him.

After thinking about all of that, my fishing trip lost some of its luster.

PART III

LAUGHS I'VE SHARED

21

JACK MACKAY'S ADVICE ON PUBLIC SPEAKING

By the mid-1990s, things were starting to happen for me. In my first four seasons as a coach, I had the great fortune to see our KSU teams finish in the top four nationally each year. Finally, in 1995, we won our first national championship.

Over the summer of 1995, I wanted to see if our success could help our program get some endorsement opportunities —you know, free stuff. So after doing a little research, I called Kaye MacKay.

I had the pleasure to work for Kaye when she was the collegiate representative for Louisville Slugger. I was so excited when she took my call and ultimately took a chance on KSU softball and me. In my efforts to get a Louisville Slugger contract, I offered to name my son after her husband. Little does Blake Whitlock know, but for several months, preceding his birth, he was referred to as "Little Jack."

Kaye was a trailblazer for us college softball coaches. She opened many of the doors we now enjoy walking through on a daily basis. Professionally, she was and remains my *fairy godmother*. My life in coaching has allowed me to live out a kid's dream, and Kaye MacKay's faith in me has played a major role in that.

Using our Louisville Slugger equipment, we repeated as national champions in 1996.

After winning the nationals twice, I suppose a curiosity started to arise within the softball world as to how we were doing things down in Kennesaw. I started getting invitations to speak at local and regional clinics and camps. It was so weird to have other coaches wanting to hear about what we did and how we did it. Then...

Kaye's call one morning in September of 1996 would prove to be a career changer. She asked me to speak at a luncheon she was hosting at the upcoming National Fastpitch Coaches Association (NFCA) Convention in New Orleans.

Kaye's account of the *request* differs from mine. I maintain that she called and asked me to speak at the convention. She claims, "I begged her like a baby" for a chance to speak. Feel free to believe whichever version you wish—but since I'm telling the story, I'd appreciate it if you'd believe mine.

As I was listening to her invitation, my self-esteem was going through the roof. I thought to myself, "I've arrived." The audience at that NFCA event was going to easily be the largest group I had ever addressed. I was truly honored, until Kaye gave me the details.

Kaye gave me the assignment to briefly speak at the luncheon about fielding gloves. I told myself, "It's simply an endorsement thing, no big deal." Then, she informed me with whom I was going to share the stage: **Mike Candrea**. That scared me to death. Let me explain.

My professional hero was (and still is) Mike Candrea. For my money, he's the best that ever coached our game! When I broke into the sport, Coach Candrea was hitting his stride at the University of Arizona. His reputation as a teacher of the game was crossing the country. I read any and everything I could get my hands on that was written by or about him. It was through his writings and presentations that I began to gain confidence as a coach and teacher of the game.

So here I go. I was going to speak on the same stage and at the same luncheon as the Master.

After a month of not being able to eat, I convinced myself I was not going to be intimidated. I was going to get up there and do what I do. It was going to be a chance of a lifetime, and I was going to enjoy it. And I did...up until 20 minutes before the luncheon started.

The event was to start at noon, and I got there early. As I walked through the door of the banquet room, I walked directly into Jack MacKay—husband of Kaye—a technological genius, and one of the bluntest people I have ever met.

I said, "Hello, Mr. MacKay." He replied, "Name's Jack." Then he asked me, "Do you know how the hell to get out of this place?" I said, "Yes sir, I'm sorry—I didn't mean to be too early." He said, "No damn it. I mean, show me how to get outside. I need to smoke a cigarette."

As we walked down the hall of the hotel, not a word was said. During that brief stroll, any confidence I had talked myself into having in the weeks leading into the convention decided to leave the state of Louisiana.

Jack MacKay is intimidating. He was then, he is now. Eventually, we reached the end of the hall and went outside into an alley. Jack had not said a single word during the entire walk.

After taking several drags off his cigarette, without talking, he then gave me the best advice on public speaking I have ever received. Jack MacKay said, "Now, look, when you get up there...say what ya' have to say and sit down. *They're comin' to see Candrea, not you. So don't take long.*" As the final bits of my self-esteem bled onto that alleyway, I muttered, "OK," and we walked back down the hallway, again without speaking. As we re-entered the luncheon hall, I was very proud of myself for not crying.

Once back inside, I picked up one of the event's programs. When I opened it and looked, I nearly swallowed my tongue. Whoever set the agenda had Coach Candrea speaking BEFORE me. Now, I knew that I was a fairly decent speaker, but I also knew that *Whitlock does not follow Candrea on a stage.*

I pointed out the obvious mistake to Jack. He handled it with the same grace that he'd used when he informed me of my role at the luncheon, "We ain't changin' a damn thing. Just get up there and do it and don't worry about it."

"Don't worry" he says. Well, the word *worry* doesn't really do justice to the place my frail little ego was visiting. However, I convinced myself to do as I was told.

I sat down at my assigned seat, and up walked Coach Mike Candrea. I stood up to meet him. He was very gracious. As it happened, the seating arrangement saw me seated between Jack and Coach Candrea. So as we ate lunch, there was the typical chitchat—well, maybe not typical. Jack and Coach talked, and I sat there in the middle. My contributions to the conversation were nodding a lot, trembling, and trying to not wet my pants.

As the meal wound down, I started to break into a flop sweat. I had my professional hero, who I had just met, to my right and Jack to my left. And my lone thought was, "Do not make an ass of yourself and, for God's sake, be brief!"

When the meal was over (of which I ate nothing), Kaye rose from her seat, welcomed everyone, and introduced Coach Candrea. He then spoke for about five minutes regarding softball bats and new designs/technology. He was quite good. Kaye then returned to the podium to introduce me.

When she finished, I promptly got up and said the following:

"I am pretty sure that you guys did not come to hear me

speak. Louisville Slugger has a new line of fielding gloves out, y'all be sure to go by their booth and check them out. Thank you." I then sat down.

The crowd roared with laughter. And, as Kaye was closing the luncheon, Jack MacKay leaned over and said to me, "That's a great job!" That day I learned a valuable lesson. It's something I will always carry with me.

It doesn't matter who you are or what you've accomplished, there's always someone who wishes that you'd just be brief, then shut up. Thanks, Jack.

* * *

Keeping my speeches brief just like Jack taught me.

In the years since that luncheon, Mike Candrea has provided me opportunities to share the stage with him countless times at camps and coaching clinics all over the world, and I have never forgotten what I was taught in New Orleans back in 1996.

"They're comin' to see Candrea, not you. So don't take long." The only difference is today I always make certain I am the opening act.

22

WORKING FOR THE KING

I t was only a few months after our introduction in New Orleans that the paths of Mike Candrea and mine crossed again. This time it was in Oklahoma City. It was August (1997) during the Gold Nationals. For those of you who are not familiar with the softball world, the ASA (Amateur Softball Association of America) Gold Nationals is a collegiate softball coach feeding frenzy and the national championship tournament for the highest level of summer travel teams.

I had driven over to one of the three unstrategically located complexes being used. Those who govern summer softball amuse themselves by scattering the 60 to 70 teams that make up a tournament field at two or three parks that are usually 20 to 90 miles apart.

As an aside, and though it's only a theory, it is my belief that there must be some type of bylaw in the governing body's constitution stating there must be heavy, ongoing road construction in a city before it can be considered as a host for any tournament.

After I had driven to one of the complexes to watch a player I was recruiting, I bumped into Coach Candrea. I could not believe it, but he actually remembered me. We had a brief but good conversation. As I was about to leave, he said, "Hey Scott, I have a coaching clinic in Tucson each October. Why don't you come down? I think it would be good for you." I promptly replied, "If there's any way I can, I'd love to." He said "Good," and that was that.

As I was going over to the game I was there to see, I thought to myself, "Wow, I just got a personal invitation from *the man* himself to come, listen, and learn at one of his clinics. I hope that I can scrape up enough money from the budget to go." The remainder of that particular recruiting trip was uneventful, and I returned home proud of my invitation and hopeful of going.

About five weeks after my return to Kennesaw, the telephone rang in my office. "Hello." "Scott?" "Yes." "Mike Candrea." "Hello, Coach this is truly a surprise," I replied. He then said, "Scott, I was wondering if you'd given any more thought to coming out to my clinic in October?"

Before I responded, I thought to myself, "This guy really pushes his clinics. I wonder if he calls everyone he meets and strong-arms them for an attendance commitment?" I then said to him, "Well Coach, I'd love to, but I really don't know. If I can squeeze the money out of my budget, I'll be there." He laughed. I thought he was making fun of my budget. After he stopped, he said "No, you *dumb shit* (which must be a term of endearment in Arizona, because he uses it frequently with me), I want you to *speak* at the thing. I pay *you* to come out." I quickly accepted his invitation and hung up. It was immediately after hanging up that I first experienced, what I call, *the feeling*.

The feeling is a horrible, uncomfortable sensation that I get deep in my gut every time I speak to a group when Mike Candrea is in the room. Let me explain it this way: Have you ever felt like the dumbest kid in a chemistry class who is standing at the chalkboard, trying to scratch out a formula, while Albert Einstein is sitting on the front row with a pad and pen? That's how I feel each time I speak at a coaching clinic when working for Coach Candrea.

Mike Candrea is now a close friend and has graciously opened countless doors for me within the industry. I am a welcome, regular guest at his home. Our wives have become friends; but in 1997 he was Mike "Freaking" Candrea—the greatest teacher of the game of softball that the world has seen.

Editor's Note: Mike Candrea has won 1,500+ games as the head softball coach for the University of Arizona—including eight national championships. He has been named NCAA National Coach of the Year four times and has won a Gold Medal and Silver Medal as head coach of the U.S. Olympic softball team. In 1996, he was inducted into the National Fastpitch Coaches Association Hall of Fame.

"The King," Mike Candrea

Anyway, back to the story of my first experience of working

with him. I flew into Tucson on a Friday morning, the third week of October 1997. Coach Candrea sent his student manager to the airport to pick me up—that's how *important* I was. The young man drove me to the hotel, saw to it that I was checked in and gave me walking directions to Coach's office and the softball field.

After unpacking, I walked over to Coach's office, to say "hello," and thank him for the opportunity. He was gracious; I was nauseous. I started to get *the feeling*. Before leaving, I asked if I could come to his team's practice. "Of course," he said. I then left his office—without throwing up.

The clinic started that night. I was scheduled to speak second. My topic was outfield play. I had my outline, was well prepared, and was terrified. Every public speaker knows to remain calm, stay focused, and to not get distracted while on stage. I felt that I was pretty good at sticking to task while presenting and would do fine. I knew I had a few things going for me:

1. It was only a 45-minute block
2. I am a decent outfield coach
3. Because of my thick Southern drawl, most of the attendees would view me as a curiosity

I was confident that I'd pull it off, until...

After the first speaker finished, Coach Candrea went on stage and gave me a generous introduction and nearly everyone politely clapped as I went on to the stage. Once up there, I thanked everyone for the warm recognition and was about to start when I noticed that Candrea took a seat on an aisle, up front. To make matters worse, he opened a notebook and got out a pen. I do not remember much about the presentation—after seeing that Mike Candrea was about to take notes while I spoke, I kind of blacked out.

At dinner that night, I told Coach Candrea just how horrible it was to have him sitting on the front row while I spoke. After a brief chuckle, he replied, *"So you think that you would have sounded smarter if I would have sat in the back?"*

For the record, I must have done OK during that 45 minutes of personal terror. That speech has led to countless opportunities for Coach Candrea and me to share speaker's platforms all over our country. It is always a great pleasure to serve as his *opening act*—but today I will not start if he is in the room. I will no longer allow *The King* to look over this dumb kid's shoulder —I hate that feeling. He thinks it's funny.

Maybe it is funny. After all, who am I to argue with *The King*?

23

"COACH, YOU'RE GOING TO HAVE A PROBLEM."

I have made a living being sensible enough to not attempt to do something I can't do. I have also been a strong advocate of *delegating, staying out of the way,* and not *micromanaging.* However, I have never allowed being an advocate of those beliefs to ever get in the way of failing to do the former and often doing the latter. Let me tell you about a day when I proved both claims in a single swoop.

One afternoon in the spring of 1992, I took it upon myself to go out and help my then-assistant, Don McKinlay, water our field. Don was in charge of field maintenance. He kept our playing surface immaculate, and spent countless hours mowing and edging. Before we installed an irrigation system, he found creative ways to water it.

One of his most creative ways involved a fire hydrant up on the hill off our third base side, a couple hundred feet of fire hose (the old cloth kind) and the wrench that could turn on the hydrant. I never asked Don where he got the hose, the nozzle, or the wrench, but then I figured that I did not need to know—I mean, why should we both go to jail?

It was a lot of work to water that field with a fire hose. For anyone who hasn't had the pleasure of utilizing a 200-foot, illegally acquired, length of fire hose, there's a lot of pressure and power in those things and you'd better be careful. If you are not, an arrogant head coach might get hurt.

As I mentioned, I went out to *assist* Don in watering the field. Once there, superior management skills kicked in and I quickly started to make suggestions. *Why don't you..., Wouldn't it be better...., How come...* The normally patient Don began to grunt a bit and show signs of resentment towards my suggestions. Until that day, I never knew Don was so resistant to *constructive suggestions*. I am not sure the field would have ever gotten watered that day if I had not yielded to him and we would have probably had to get a new hose. At one point in our debate on field irrigation, he came up with a *new place* to attach the hose. If we had used that suggestion, I sure would have walked funny, and it would have taken *forever* to water the field.

When we finally made the decision to go ahead and use the hydrant (and thankfully not Don's new suggestion), we hooked it up and attached the nozzle. He asked me to get the wrench and go up to the hydrant to turn it on. I denied this request: "I want to run the hose. Go turn it on." Oops. He consented and went up the hill with the wrench and with, what I believe was, a sadistic grin on his face.

Once up the hill, he yelled to me as I stood at the pitcher's mound—hose in hand.

> Don: *"I'm going to turn it on now."*
> Me: *"OK."*
> *I grabbed the hose firmly and aimed. When he*
> *turned it on, the water began to erupt from*
> *nozzle, but it wasn't getting the coverage I felt*
> *was acceptable.*
> Me: *"Turn it up."*

> *Don (now yelling): "Coach, I can't turn it up. You'll*
> *have a problem."*
> *Me: "What kind of problem?"*
> *Don: "The pressure's fairly strong."*
> *Me: "Fairly strong? Just turn it up! I'm not going to be*
> *out here all day!"*
> *Don (now pleading): "Coach, we are going to have*
> *problems."*
> *Me: "Don, TURN THE WATER UP! "OK?"*
> *Don (now frustrated): "FINE!"*

He did. And, we *did* have a problem. When he cranked that damn hydrant up higher, all the water on the East Coast rushed to the head of the hose I was holding, and I was off to the races.

From between the mound and shortstop, I began to round the bases in reverse. I first landed near second base—that hose dribbled me like a basketball. When the hose lifted me from second, I then landed somewhere between second and first base, and then again on first. During all of this, I was hanging on for dear life, drowning, and figuring out if there is any way that I could save my dignity.

All the while, Don, safely on the hill, was laughing. I was cussing and water was going everywhere. At one point, during all of this, I fired Don. I then concluded, *to hell with dignity*, and quickly rehired him. I then screamed the first assignment of his reinstatement to him, "CUT IT OFF, CUT IT OFF, CUT IT OFF!" He took his sweet time, but he finally did.

When it was all over, I had lost the hide off my right forearm, most of the skin from two fingers of my left hand and had irrigated most of northwest Georgia. To this day, I am scared of the garden hoses at home and will not go near them. But I did learn a lesson.

* * *

If you hire someone to do a job, and if they do it well, and if he tells you that "you might have a problem if you..." **LISTEN TO HIM!** Or, at least wear gloves and a long-sleeved shirt! Better yet, stay out of the damn way and let him do the job that he was hired to do.

24

BAD OYSTERS ARE NO JOKE

One of my closest friends is Jess Dannelly, a 6-foot-4 mountain of a teddy bear who was the softball coach at Coastal Carolina University for many years. He has a thick *low country* South Carolina brogue, broad shoulders, a big heart, and he loves good food.

Jess is the unofficial patriarch of a southern contingent of softball coaches known as *The Bubbas*. They are some of the finest, most loyal guys you could know. To be a card-carrying member of the *Bubbas* you must: 1) hail from the South; 2) weigh at least at 250 pounds; and 3) possess a sense of humor. For the record, I am not sure if I am an *honorary Bubba, a Bubba via special exemption,* or *a Bubba in waiting* (as I do not meet the weight minimum). I have never been told, but I am welcome at the meetings. So, I'm sure that I'm a *Bubba* of some kind.

Of all the *Bubbas*, Jess is the most official. He's definitely a Southerner. The weight requirement he easily makes. Regarding his sense of humor, all one needs to do is to listen to him for three minutes while he's holding court and you'll see the man loves to laugh.

If I were describing my buddy Jess to a stranger, I'd say, "If the Looney Tunes rooster, *Foghorn Leghorn*, could teach hitting, he'd be Jess Dannelly." Get the picture? I wanted to introduce Jess to you because he is one of our games' true characters and he had a supporting role in the events I am about to document.

I always enjoy spending time with my peers. The softball coaching fraternity consists of a lot of good people (*and a few southern ends of north bound donkeys*). We are so spread out across the country that we rarely convene. So, whether it's at a tournament here or a convention there, it's always great to hang out and visit with fellow coaches. One such occasion was at our coaches association's annual convention held in New Orleans in December 1996. (This is the same convention at which I made my infamous national speaking debut chronicled in chapter 20.)

At that convention, Jess and I were rooming together, and we made the rounds each night after all the official daily activities concluded. We did lots of things. One night we went to a jazz club, another we strolled up and down Bourbon Street—strictly for research purposes—and one night we, along with a few other coaches, invaded the Acme Oyster House. That evening we sat and howled at each other, watched football, and had our fill of *raw* oysters.

Now, any *real* Southern man loves to partake in the epicurean delight provided by digesting raw oysters. It's a badge of honor to put one of those gels of dirt and fish waste on a cracker, splash some Tabasco on it, and choke it down—hopefully without reversing engines. I must admit, at one time I loved those things and would eat a dozen or so any time I could. No more.

The night at the Acme Oyster House, Jess and I had our fill and then some. I, a true middleweight, made the mistake of trying to stay with a proven heavyweight. By the time Jess and I left that joint, I was moaning and groaning. He, of course, was laughing. When we finally got back to the hotel, I made the same vow regarding raw oysters that many a drinker has made, "Lord, if you'll help me through this, I'll never..."

We awoke the next morning, the date of our departure, and I felt much better. It seemed that the Almighty had heard and accepted the terms of my pledge. I said my goodbyes to Jess and headed for home having learnt a great lesson and with one less item off my personal menu.

The following week was hectic. I had to get caught up at the office, and I had to prepare for my second big public speaking appearance. The weekend after New Orleans, I was booked to speak at a coaches clinic in Nashville, Tennessee. Cheri Kempf was the clinic's host.

* * *

For those of you who do not know my friend Cheri Kempf, she is a former world-class pitcher who at one time was a highly sought after pitching instructor. She's also a tremendous business person. She was the owner of *Club K*, a then trend-setting instructional facility for softball players. Located in the greater-Nashville area, Club K had emerged from humble beginnings to become an endeared and highly-respected entity within our profession. At any given time, more than 1,400 young women are under the tutelage of the very capable instructors of Club K. All told, Club K alumnus have received over $6 million in scholarships. Today, Cheri Kempf is both an excellent color commentator of softball and is the commissioner of the NPF— the U.S.'s only women's professional softball league. *You're welcome for the plug, C.K.*

* * *

As previously stated, I was booked to speak at Cheri's clinic just one week removed from my oyster binge in *The Big Easy*. On that Friday morning, my wife, Susan, and I climbed into our car and headed north from our Marietta, Georgia, home toward *Music City, U.S.A.* From Marietta to Nashville is about a three-and-a-half-hour drive. We left early and were going to take our time. We stopped in Chattanooga, Tennessee, for lunch and continued north over Monteagle (a small mountain). I have never known why the folks of Tennessee couldn't call it *Mount* Eagle or Eagle *Mountain.* Why *Mont?* I guess that will always be one of the great mysteries of that charming state.

As we went along our way toward Nashville, I began to feel poorly. I could not decide if it was lunch or what, but something was starting to kick me around. It got so bad that I had to pull over and let Susan drive. While I laid against the passenger side window of our front seat, she drove us into Nashville. Once there, she checked us into the nice hotel at which Cheri had reserved our room. With my health in rapid decline, I staggered to our room while Susan unpacked the car. I immediately went to bed for a nap in hopes of rallying before going to dinner.

That night there was a dinner for the speakers and attendees of the clinic. Cheri hosted it at the Opryland Hotel. Legendary Olympic Softball Coach Ralph Raymond was to deliver a keynote speech. Though I had never met him, I'm an admirer of Coach Raymond and was anxious to meet him.

When I awoke from my nap I quickly discovered there was to be no rally. My head was swimming, my tongue was twice its normal thickness (and coated) plus I had a fever of somewhere between 102 and 173 degrees. I immediately told Susan I thought that I was coming down with the flu or something. She then went to a drugstore, got some meds and I took them. We then got ready for the dinner. I took a hot shower to help ease my aches and pains. Then, I dressed. Susan opted to drive to the Opryland, since she noticed that I was seeing double and referring to her using my ex-wife's name (*that was pretty much it for the bedside manner on that trip*).

When we arrived for dinner, Susan dragged me to the banquet hall where I sweltered then froze during dinner and then hallucinated all the way back to the hotel. I honestly remember nothing of that evening.

Now y'all, I will be the first to admit that I am a wuss and a poor sick patient. I whine, gripe, and feign death over a hangnail, so you can imagine my mental state during all of this. I was sick as I'd ever been, but even in my pathetic state I knew come Saturday morning, I had to do three, one-hour talks at that clinic and I was not about to *call in sick*.

When we woke up the next morning, I was no better. I struggled through breakfast and dressed. Susan then drove me over to Club K where I was to speak. My first topic of the day was outfield play. I remember being introduced and starting, and I recall concluding, other than that—nothing. I must have done a hell of a job though, because as I was staggering through the room after my speech, I happened past Coach Raymond who had come in at some point. When we made eye contact, he held up the OK signal and said in his New England voice, "Great job, Scotty."

I really wish I could remember what I said that day. If it was good enough to get a "Great job, Scotty" from a legend, it could not have been all bad. Maybe one day, when I see him again, I'll ask Coach Raymond what I said. The remainder of that weekend was more of the same. After I struggled through two more sessions, Susan drove us home Sunday morning. While going home I told her "If I am not better or dead tomorrow, I'm going to the doctor."

The next morning, I felt no better. True to my word, I went to the doctor. Our family physician is a portly fellow named Dr. David Williams. He is a good man with a keen wit and good old common sense. After he allowed me to tell him what I was feeling and given me a once over, he said, "I'll be right back." I always hate it when a doctor examines you and then immediately leaves the room. I feel as if they've left to call one of their doctor buddies to tell them, "You ain't gonna believe what I got over here at my place."

In this case, Dr. Williams was only gone briefly and returned with a couple of papers in his hand. "Scott, when's the last time you were on the Gulf Coast?" I thought to myself, "What a hell of a question. I'm sitting here dying and this bum wants to talk fishing?" I then responded aloud, "I was in New Orleans about 10 days ago. Why?" He said, "Have any raw shellfish while you were down there?" I returned, "Yeah, but like I said Doc, I was home at least a week before I started feeling bad." To which he replied, "This (referring to the papers) is an alert we received about three weeks ago. It warns of bacteria that are running rampant in shellfish in the Gulf of Mexico. That's what wrong with you." He went on, "What it does is, it attacks the lining of your stomach and eats it away. I can write you a prescription and fix you right up."

Whew. What a relief. I felt like a giant weight had been lifted off my body. I was so happy to know that it wasn't an ulcer or worse. It was only bacteria, and a few pills later it would all be gone. As Dr. Williams wrote a prescription, I joked, "Doc this thing was *like a hangover that hung on.*" He laughed and said, "I know what you mean." He then seriously said, "I am glad we can laugh about it, because if you had not come in we'd not be laughing." I responded, "Would I have gotten worse?" He said, "Nope, dead."

Well, the weight that had been lifted landed right back on my skinny shoulders. "Dead?" I asked with a noticeable quiver. "Oh, yeah. Anytime you eat anything raw from the ocean you're rolling the dice." I left the doctor's office both relieved and frightened. I was happy we had caught it, but I was terrified of what nearly happened.

* * *

That ordeal taught me several things:

- If you're sick don't procrastinate—go to the doctor!
- Sometimes you do your best work when you're *playing hurt*—remember my "Great Job Scotty"—*I still wish I knew what I said that day.*
- Never try to keep up with a *Bubba* when he's eating.

And finally, yet most importantly...**bad oysters are no joke!**

25

"SCOTT, I THINK THAT I COULD'VE TOOK HER."

THE DAY FLOYD GOT PUNCHED

Now, I have seen some sights in my years at the ballpark. I have even made a sight of myself on occasion. Of 'em all, the story I am about to share just might have been the funniest thing I ever saw. Everything you are about to read actually happened.

Dyan Mueller was the first great pitcher we had at KSU. Over the first three seasons (1991-93) of our program, she was our heart and soul. A very serious, dignified young woman, she was everything you wanted in a leader. Oft times, she would help her less experienced teammates learn about the game— she'd even teach her head coach an occasional lesson (see chapter 15).

Dyan grew up at the ballpark. Both she and her brother were very accomplished athletes in Calgary, Alberta, Canada. Their biggest fan was their dad, Floyd.

Floyd Mueller is one of a kind. He was a businessman by profession, but he's actually a walking entertainment center. The guy can talk sports with anyone, and I mean talk intelligently. If you gave him a piano and a microphone, he could entertain any audience. I believe he knows the words to nearly every song ever written. Among his many talents, my personal favorites are his quick wit and his terrific storytelling skills. When Floyd is holding court, there will be no one in the room who is not laughing. He is truly a gifted, special person. None of these things about Floyd Mueller have one thing to do with this story—except maybe his quick wit. Here we go.

* * *

Our first season of fastpitch play (1991) was remarkable. We took an inexperienced group of 12 slowpitch players, added four experienced players and carved out a 41-11 record. That team advanced to the NAIA World Series where it finished fourth. Not bad for a first-year team by anyone's standards.

As we started year number two (1992), we added a fine recruiting class and were optimistic about the season—and we had a good one. When our regular season opened, we picked up where we left off in 1991. We played good defense, our offense was drastically improved by our new additions, and Dyan's pitching had us in every game. The season went along very well. We won our conference, advanced to the playoffs, and to the World Series.

The 1992 NAIA World Series was held in Pensacola, Florida. There were several very good teams there that year. We knew we'd have our hands full. Oklahoma City University, coached by the underrated Phil McSpadden, was there, as was Pacific Lutheran from Washington state. Huntingdon College of Montgomery, Alabama, who had one of the game's most intimidating pitchers, Debbie Sonnenberg, was a favorite as well. It was a deep tournament field.

As the 16-team event opened, we got off to a good start. We won our first two games and set up a winner's bracket semifinal game against Huntingdon and Sonnenberg. Debbie Sonnenberg was (and still is) a hard-throwing lefty from Edmonton,

Alberta, Canada. She was a four-time NAIA All-American and an Olympian. While competing against her, I always admired her fearless approach. She could make the ball move and was not afraid to come inside. Her willingness to throw inside earned her a reputation as a pitcher who'd hit opponents on purpose. I never bought into that notion, and though I know many of my colleagues felt differently, I always attributed her high number of HBPs (batters hit by pitch) to the fact that she threw hard and threw in.

After finishing her playing career, she became a fine pitching coach. She's worked with Auburn University and is currently at Mercer University. In between those stints, she spent a few years working for a university located just north of Atlanta—whose coach really hopes that you are enjoying this book (especially if you paid for it).

When we squared off with Huntingdon, Sonnenberg was dominant. Her pitches were simply blowing us away. In the top of the fourth inning, with Huntingdon up 1-0, Dyan Mueller led off the inning. Not only was she our top pitcher, she was one of our best hitters. Sonnenberg's first pitch to "Dy" ran in and hit her right hand—you know, the one she throws with—her right @#$^ing hand. Dyan fell in immense pain. Her right hand was clearly damaged. She, of course, had to come out of the game. Considering Sonneberg's reputation, all hell broke loose in the stands.

* * *

Our fans started screaming at Sonnenberg. Huntingdon's fans started screaming back. In the middle of this was Floyd. He was livid. Now I must confess, the Huntingdon crowd was much more adept at yelling than our crowd—after all they were from Alabama.

As the game went along, and as Huntingdon continued to

lead, the Alabamans got louder and louder. Their efforts were being led by the mothers of two of the Huntingdon players. I will not identify the two athletes because both are currently fine collegiate coaches within the state of Alabama (one works where Bear Bryant once did and the other works in Huntsville, but I will not divulge their identity). *I love you Les and Van.*

We lost the game to Huntingdon and worse we lost Dyan. Our spiritual leader, and best pitcher, was gone—fractured hand. We were on our way to the to the loser's bracket with only our number-two thrower. We won our first loser's-bracket game. Our little number two, Kena Wood, did a great job. That kid could not throw hard enough to break glass, but she nibbled and wiggled herself through it. We then beat a very good West Florida team to get us into the "loser's-bracket finals" and to set up a meeting with guess who? **Huntingdon, Sonnenberg** and the **Anarchists** (I mean fans). This is where Floyd's adventures begin.

Floyd Mueller is a pure Canadian sports fan—by that I mean he loves his sports and booze. I have never known a Canadian sports fan who didn't like to enhance their game watching experience with a few spirits. Floyd is no different. Though I never confirmed this, I heard reports that in between games (and some innings) Floyd would visit his car in the parking lot and partake of the offerings at his own private concession stand. Remember that.

Even before we started the game, the crowd was nipping at each other—early on Floyd was just nipping. There was truly electricity in the air. There were only three teams left in the tournament, our two and Pacific Lutheran who was waiting to play the winner, so all eyes were on our game.

* * *

When little Kena went out there to battle, every move she made was greeted by some type of jeer by the fans from Montgomery. When I left the safety of our first base dugout to go over to coach third, I got it, too. Now, I am an old-school baseball player who is accustomed to, and am pretty fair at giving, verbal cheap shots—so, I was in heaven. I mean, a big game at the national championship tournament with a hostile crowd? It just doesn't get any better than that. Our players were unfazed by anything coming from outside the fence, but our fans were not so aloof. They quickly grew weary of all the noise from behind the third base side of the backstop and were becoming a bit more vocal than usual.

Kena did her best, and after three innings we found ourselves in a 0-0 game. The crowd words and exchanges were getting sharper. The Huntingdon faithful, led by *Big Ma-Ma*, had their A-game going. If I had not been coaching that game, I would have loved to have taken a shot at the title by verbally squaring off with her, but alas, the game.

Entering the sixth inning the score was still 0-0. Then a rally started. We got a bloop single, followed by a walk. Sonnenberg, for the first time in the week-long tournament looked human. I then gambled a bit, and double-stole second and third. Then we got it—a big hit to plate two runs. When that happened, the stands went nuts. Our crowd showed they could be just as obnoxious as our neighbors from one state over. Floyd, who by then had been to his *personal* concession stand numerous times, was the loudest. In the mist of all this, Floyd had made his way over to the third base side of the field. Once there, he positioned himself behind the Queen Bee herself, and started screaming, "LET'S GO KENNESAW! GO KENNESAW!" In less than a heartbeat, the spirited female fan from Alabama stood up, turned, and punched Floyd in the face. I witnessed the event from the safety of the third-base coaching box. I could not believe what I had just seen, but I knew I had just seen it. People immediately got in between them and quickly broke it up. Floyd's assailant sat back down, Floyd returned to more friendly territory (with his glasses dangling from his left ear). It was funny as hell.

When we went out to play defense in the bottom of the sixth, I had Dyan crying in our dugout (due to the punch), Floyd laughing (his glasses still dangling), leading all the yelling from our stands, a lady across the way looking to kill Floyd, and a two-run lead. Little Kena went out there and made the runs stand up. We won. We beat a great team, their great pitcher, and went on to play for the national title.

We only had 20 minutes between games and I had made my way down the right field to put together a lineup for the championship game. Suddenly, here comes Floyd, with his glasses still dangling. He came a yelling, "Whitlock, you're a genius (his drinking had obviously not yet affected his ability to evaluate people's mental capacity). I can't believe you double-stole. What a move. And those hits, what a game!"

I quickly thanked him. Then I had to ask, "Floyd, did you have a little trouble with the big gal?" His response was quick and as serious as it could be, "**Yeah, I should not have gone over there. But, I'll tell you one thing. Scott, I think that I could have took her. If they had not have got in between us. I'da took her.**"

Those series of events did not teach me one thing. They were just some of the funniest set of circumstances you'll ever see. By the way, we lost 3-2 to Pacific Lutheran in the finals, but I was so proud of our club.

Oh yeah, *Floyd, the only way that you could have "**took her**" is if, after she got through beating your butt, she had forced you to "**take her**" to your private concession stand for drinks.*

AFTERWORD

In Appreciation
We Ain't the Brady Bunch, but We Ain't Bad

It was not my intent to write specifically about my immediate family. It is difficult for me to talk about them. Despite what most think, I am a big wuss and talking about my family makes me very emotional. Nonetheless, as this project has unfolded, I found that it would be incomplete if I did not. I realized if I am going to write a book that is faintly career related, I must at least introduce those who have sacrificed the most in order for me to enjoy so much.

Make no mistake about it—there is no married coach, no coach with children who has not required that both his/her spouse and children make sacrifices. Additionally (*at least in my case*), grandparents are asked to do more than they should. I asked so much (too much) of all of them as I chased my coaching rainbow.

My kids grew up with their dad usually gone, coming home, or getting ready to leave. My wife was a single, married parent. She had to be both mom and dad. Pop and Granny were called upon, due to my absence, all too often. Looking back, I feel so badly about it and it is hard to talk about, so I usually do not.

As I finish these essays in early 2019, my immediate family consists of my wife Susan, daughter Lacey, son Blake, son-in-law *What's his Name*, granddaughter Blair "Boogie" Bass (who has a brother on the way), and two moms Dora (biological) and Grace (wife of Linwood and gift from God).

My family is unique, but it is no more dysfunctional than anyone else's. We ain't the *Brady Bunch*, but we ain't bad. Now, I am not going to delve into long sappy paragraphs, nor am I going to air any dirty laundry. I enjoy keeping my personal life just that—personal. I do think the people who were affected the most by my professional pursuits are at least entitled to be introduced as I write. During my career I asked so much of them, so this is the least I can do. Therefore, I just need to suck it up and write.

First, let me explain as to why I consider myself to have two moms. Dora Thompson is my biological mother. She is known to her grandkids as "Mi-Mi." When she had me, she was Dora Whitlock. She and my dad had me when they were both young. As I said, I will not dwell on details in this chapter, but my childhood was a little different. I spent most of my childhood living in my grandparents' home. My parents had a home 100 yards behind it. After 18+ years of trying, Mom could not handle living with my dad anymore—he was an alcoholic. Her leaving scarred everyone involved, but (now I know) it did not scar us any greater than the toll of what we all went through living with daddy's demons.

Ma-Ma (Mi-Mi) and Me

When Mom left, I was already in college, but my three siblings were not. They were left to be raised for the most part by my grandparents. I could not believe she could just leave everyone behind and go away. I was angry she had left my grandparents to raise three young kids. Nearly 40 years later, I can confess that I did not handle it as well as I could have, but at the time it was what it was. Luckily, there is a happy ending.

Time and maturity allowed me to grow. I recalled that my Granny had taught me the basic Christian principles—two of which are forgiveness and not being judgmental. I also did not want my children to grow up seeing their dad and grandmother estranged. Mom and I patched things up. Today, we are very much in each other's world. The past is just that, the past. We both forgave and forgot. I am glad it happened and happy we made things right before my kids were born.

Mi-Mi is one of the best cooks of genuine, authentic Southern cuisine that I know. Her green beans are to die for. No matter whether its fried chicken, country fried steak, roast beef, creamed corn, or *real* macaroni and cheese, my mom can cook! She does not know what a gluten is and doesn't care. She still uses lard (yeah, I said lard), and she believes that anything other than real butter is some kind of government conspiracy. Mi-Mi still cooks *real food*. Now, some sophisticates might raise a nose to *real food*. "Oh, that's bad for you," they might say. SHUT UP. Mi-Mi's food is good to eat and it's good for a son's soul.

Now, as to my other mom who I truly believe was a gift from God Almighty. In 1985 when I arrived at Kennesaw College my personal life was in disarray. My first marriage was strained and eventually failed. I was trying to start a career as a coach but was floundering personally. It was during that time I met a little 5-foot-nothing busybody named Grace Stuckey Register. "Ma-Ma" worked in the accounting area of our school's business office. As fate would have it, she had the duty of making certain that a flock of newly hired coaches kept their work-related finances in order.

Ma-Ma must have been prodded from above, because she took an almost immediate interest in a 24-year-old coach who was a long way from Bostwick, Georgia, and who was in need of someone to be a maternal influence. Man was I lucky. In short order, she sized me up and (along with her husband Linwood) took me in as one of their own. It has been that way ever since. She is not *like family*, she *is* family. She is a grandmother to my children and continues (in her 89th year) to be a Ma-Ma to me.

Ma-Ma and Pop (Linwood) saved my career, not to mention my life. They helped me regain balance when my personal life was spiraling toward self-destruction. Ma-Ma was (and remains) unafraid to tell me what I need to hear. She filled in for my Granny who had made me go to church and to try to do what is right.

Grace Register can talk 1,000 miles per hour. She will ask anyone any question. She is the epitome of a little old Southern lady. My children adore her. She loves my daughter and spoiled my son. As I mentioned, she is now 89 and slowing a bit, but she still has all the advice I could possibly want (and then some). I thank God daily for his Grace (Register).

Lacey Marie Whitlock Bass is my oldest child. She is married to *What's his Name* (Blayne Bass) and is the mother of my wife's favorite person, Blair Kennedy "Boogie" Bass. And, as of March 22, 2019, at 9 a.m. (if not sooner) she'll also be the mom of Wyatt Linwood Bass. Lacey is a spoiled *daddy's girl*. She is smart. She took four years of French in college for no apparent reason and today she is a very good 12th grade English Literature teacher. She is also hard headed. Wonder where she gets that? Lacey was born to my first wife and me. That marriage ended very early in Lacey's life. Lacey's mom and I parted on reasonable terms and committed ourselves to working together in rearing our daughter.

I wish that I could take at least some credit, but it was thanks to Kellye Whitlock (first wife) and Susan Whitlock that Lacey Marie Whitlock "Tater" Bass grew up to be a fantastic woman. Though I am very proud of her, I cannot be too puffy-chested about it because I was gone most of the time. Fortunately for me, Lacey was always a coach's kid. So, she knew nothing else but that type of life. She has always given me pardon when I was away or missed a birthday party. I love me some Tater.

As Lacey grew into a teenager, she, Kellye, and Susan successfully managed to keep me out of the loop when it came to most of her social life. For some reason, they felt I might overreact if I learned that some young man had hurt my daughter's feelings or be too quick to judge a young suitor's appearance. I have no idea why they had such little confidence in my ability to be reasonable and fair in regard to coping with some punk-ass teenage boy wanting to date my only daughter.

Upon her graduating from college, Lacey started her professional career as a teacher. Then it wasn't too long before I started hearing whispers between Lacey and Susan about some

Georgia State student that she was dating. It was inevitable I guess. I was forced to meet *What's his Name*. I did not know *What's his Name* at all. I had no feud going with his folks, he wasn't ugly, and he was polite and respectful. Much to my dismay, he made it very difficult for me to find something wrong with him. Eventually, he married my baby girl.

For the record, Blayne Bass is a great young man. He loves my daughter very much. He is unafraid of work, is a great father to my granddaughter, and will be for my future grandson. I witnessed him do manual labor for several months to earn a living to care for his family while he was searching for a job within his chosen field—that is what a *real man* does. He has my respect. I have to admit that I love the kid. He continues to grow on me. In fact, my faith in him has grown so much that I am no longer reluctant to tell people that my son-in-law is a high school marching band director (yeah, yeah, a marching band, there I said it). Ha, just joking. Blayne Bass is a talented educator and a fine musician. I love hearing him play.

I am very proud of Mr. and Mrs. *What's his Name*. They only live two miles away and, though it is expensive, I am grateful for it. I am also grateful that they gave me a granddaughter. On July 28, 2016, the rules in my world changed. Blair Kennedy Bass was born. She is Susan Whitlock's favorite person and Susan is Blair's favorite person, so that works nicely, doesn't it?

Becoming a grandfather has been a humbling experience for me. Blair "Boogie" Bass now calls most of the shots. She has a mind of her own. Wonder where she got that, Lacey? Therefore, I have had to learn I am no longer in any way remotely in charge of anything at my house. Boogie now runs the place. And, any time that I attempt to regain any clout within my residence, she immediately turns her chief advocate loose on me— Susan "Su-Su" Whitlock, Boogie's favorite person.

Boogie is a regular guest at my house. Immediately upon entering the door she does one of two things: runs straight to

Su-Su or asks for Su-Su. Once together, they become oblivious to all others. They are in a world all their own. What's more, no one else is seemingly invited. Susan and Boogie are an undisciplined, freewheeling pair. When they are together, common sense is nowhere to be found. I am still learning to deal with it.

Robert Blakely Whitlock is my son. Currently, he is finishing college and getting ready to take on the world. Blake is a good kid. He's a brave kid. He has dared to try things I would not have ever dared to try. At a very young age, he earned his black belt in karate. He was a leader in Lassiter High School's ROTC program. While in high school he was also a member of the Georgia Youth Symphony Orchestra as a violinist. I would have never had the guts to try such things.

More so than any of my other family members, I regret missing so much during Blake's formative years. He did not miss any opportunities due to my profession, but I missed a lot. I seemingly always had to *hear about* how he did, when it should have been my job to be there. I regret that more than I care to share.

For more than 20 years, one of my great joys has been witnessing Blake's relationship with his Granny (Grace). That little woman continues to spoil him. Blake was very young when Pop died so he was spared much of the sorrow that Lacey endured, but he played a key role as his Granny coped. Almost immediately after Pop's passing, Granny and Blake went into *business*. It was *their business* and no one else's.

Blake helped fill a hole in Ma-Ma's life that came with Pop's passing. She immersed herself into all things Blake. They had a standing Friday night sleepover on the calendar. On Saturdays he got breakfast in bed while he watched cartoons. And, you did not want to be the one who asked Granny "why did you spoil that boy so much?" Trust me on this. No one (and I mean no one) tells Grace Register anything when it comes to her "baby." Blake Whitlock is the only person I know who can get paid $50 for coming by and changing the kitchen light bulb. I have offered to do it for free and have been told bluntly to mind my own business. In the early years, Granny drove Blake to restaurants. Today, Blake drives Granny but she still pays.

As already noted, Blair "Boogie" Bass is my granddaughter. As I write, she is just short of being 4 years old. I have already shared of her and my wife's mutual admiration society. That is a constant but there is a potential storm brewing. As previously noted, Blair is about to become a big sister. It is going to be interesting to see how Blair handles the arrival of a sibling. To date, she has shown no interest in sharing the spotlight. I predict that within two weeks of her mother and little brother returning home from the hospital Blair will either 1.) Put out a contract on the new arrival or 2.) She will rent a U-Haul and move to Su-Su's house. If that happens, I honestly do not know if I will be allowed to remain a resident.

Susan Whitlock is my wife. She is perhaps the most decent person I know. I love and respect her. She is a former athlete and coach, turned college professor. Why we are married, I do not know.

- Susan is dignified. I am not.
- Susan is patient. I am not.
- Susan is soft-spoken and levelheaded. I am neither.

She raised our children with little to no help from me. Folks, on my best days I am no walk in the park, and yet she has stayed. Mrs. Whitlock has rarely complained. She has accepted and tolerated me warts and all. Susan continues to hold things together and runs our family. I do not know why. I owe her so much.

Susan and I have made it work for nearly 30 years. We share children, memories, and countless friends. I have to stop now.

As I said, I find it hard to write about my family *and this subtopic is harder than the others.*

My extended family

Well I did it. I managed to get through writing about my family without having (as we say down here) "a spell." I am a lucky man.

* * *

Ladies and gentlemen, we have a late entry...

On March 22 of 2019, my daughter Lacey and her husband, *What's his Name* gave me my first grandson. Mr. Wyatt Linwood Bass entered this world weighing 8 pounds, 1 ounce, and stood 1-foot-8 inches tall (I know that's only 20 inches but to enhance his nearly completed recruiting portfolio, I thought that listing him at 1'8" would add more pizazz). As I write, he's almost 5 days old—gotta get his name out there.

So far so good. I think that he likes me. I hope so, because I sure like him.

My grandkids Blair and Wyatt

ACKNOWLEDGMENTS

In 2007, Nancy Carey Peters, Wynelle Callaway Ruark, and Amy Snow Herndon collected, edited, and published a series of essays/accounts about life in my hometown of Bostwick, Georgia. Their book, *Old Times Here Are Not Forgotten*, is a great stroll down memory lane for those of us who come from the little town in northern Morgan County.

I was honored to be asked to provide my memories and feelings of home—the place and people who helped shaped me.

So when I decided to write this book, I felt inclined to include the essay in hopes of giving readers greater insight into who I am and where I come from.

* * *

My Upbringing

During my childhood in Bostwick, it was not uncommon in the South for grandparents to play a large role in a child's upbringing. I was one of those kids. In fact, my Granny and Pa-

Pa played a greater role in my upbringing than most grandparents did.

For the first five years of my life, my parents (**Bobby** and **Dora Whitlock**), my grandparents, and I all shared the same little two-bedroom, one-bathroom house. About the time my sister Cheryl came along in 1966, my mom and dad built their own house—directly behind Granny's and Pa-Pa's, so it was like I really never left. By the time I was an early teen, for various reasons (including my grandfather's health), I was back living with Granny and Pa-Pa.

Me in Bostwick at age 4

I am the oldest of four grandchildren, and if you believe my siblings, I was clearly Pa-Pa's favorite. From the day I was born, he showed a special interest in me. He was my hero, and everything about him was bigger than life (both virtues and faults). My grandfather had little formal education but possessed great common sense. I like to think that I have some of his instincts and people skills. I am afraid I also have his temper and impatience.

Now Granny clearly ran the show (although she let Pa-Pa think he did), and she had no favorites. She loved us all equally and a bunch. It was Granny who made certain that on Sundays we were in church, and on the other six days of the week we acted like we had listened while there.

Granny and Pa-Pa were key influences of my early life and have remained so. Everything I have achieved or become is directly due to their love and faith in me.

People of Character and Characters

When I was a boy, Bostwick was full of men and women of great character. It had its share of characters, too.

Robert C. Whitlock Sr.: My grandfather definitely fell into the "character" category. He remains the primary male influence of my life. My Pa-Pa had a complex personality. He would have made any psychologist say, "Damn." But they would have loved my Pa-Pa. He could go from laughing to cussing in a nanosecond.

Robert C. Whitlock Sr. - My Pa-Pa

If he liked you, you had a loyal friend. If you crossed him, or if you were a 1970s Republican, he could be a huge pain in the rear. (If truth be told, at times, he could be a pain in the you know where even if he liked you and you were a Democrat.) I miss him so much.

Mozelle Knight Whitlock: My grandmother was the finest person I ever knew. She was a lady of character. Now, I know a lot of people say things like that about their grandma, but my Granny was *special*.

She lived 92 years, and I was around for 42 of them. During that time, I never once saw her embarrass herself or lose her dignity. She was a devout Southern Baptist lady who never questioned what life dealt her. Granny was what people *should be*. She was Bostwick's postmaster for 37 years. Over those years, when people came to get their mail, she always greeted them with a pleasant smile and a friendly tone.

The only criticism I can recall regarding Granny was of her being too patient with Pa-Pa. She was the epitome of grace and class.

Other Folks

John Nunn: He was a school bus driver, farmer, baseball coach, and politician. He was seemingly always running for (and usually winning) some office. Additionally, he was one of my little league coaches and the first person ever to let me help him coach.

Mr. Bo and **Miss Luddie Peppers:** They owned one of the town's two gas stations. You could also get a hamburger or hot dog there.

Henry Burge: He and his wife, Miss Margaret, ran the town's other filling station. Two of their sons, Allen and Terrell, were some of my early playmates. Terrell was later my college roommate. Their gas station was more of a *full-service* facility than Mr. Bo's. Henry would fix tires, change oil, and stuff like that. Henry's gas station also served as the school bus stop for many of us.

Miss Bebe Ruark, Miss Sybil Nunn, and **Miss Margaret Burge:** These ladies gave me countless car rides to practices and ball games and many wonderful meals at their homes.

Johnny and **Mary Lill:** For my money, they were textbook examples of what parents and adults should be—real role models. They always welcomed me into their home and their lives. I love them dearly and respect them even more. Through his activity at our church, Mr. Lill taught countless young boys to water ski. Miss Mary is a lady in every sense of the word and a great mom to my friend John and his brother Ken.

Miss Velma Lill and **Miss Ruby Williams:** Miss Velma was my buddy John Lill's grandmother, and Miss Ruby was her sister. The two women shared a home close to where we lived. John and I played there many a day. John still kids me about the peanut butter and banana sandwiches that we were regularly offered—I hated them but didn't have the heart to tell Miss Velma or Miss Ruby, so I made John do it.

J.B. Ruark: J.B. Ruark made a huge impact on me. He, too, was one of my first coaches. For a good part of my childhood, he, along with his wife Louvie, trucked us boys all over the county to play baseball. He was a great coach who, unknowingly to him at the time, planted the seed of my coaching for a living. One day while I was riding with him in his truck while he dragged the infield, he told me he thought I could be a coach someday.

I am so happy that before he passed away I had a chance to thank him for the impact he had on me.

Marvin and **Gene Ruark:** They are lifelong friends of my dad and the fathers of two of my closest friends John (Marvin's boy) and Mark (Gene's son). The elder Ruarks remain like uncles to me. When I was young, they gave me a place to earn spending money and they always gave me good, common-sense advice. I will always be grateful for their encouragement and support regarding my coaching career. Their family's long, continuing friendship with me and my family is something I truly cherish and appreciate. I cried so hard when Gene died in 2016.

Irvin Lowe: Irvin Thomas Lowe, or I.T., as his wife, Joyce, calls him, is my second cousin. He and my dad grew up together. His mother, my Aunt Ruby, and my Granny were sisters. Irvin's great wit has always made me laugh. I went to car races with him beginning at age 10. His daughter April, grew up with my sister Cheryl, and his son Mark grew up with my brother Phillip. Irvin is one of a kind—a good one.

Me with Irvin and Joyce

Eleanor Knight Young (my *Aunt Ellen*): My Aunt Ellen was my Granny's youngest sister and lived next door to us until I was about 10 years old. When I was a baby, I spent a lot of time in the house owned by her and my "Ma-Ma Ginny" (my great grandmother). A daily ritual was that, after Ellen got home from work, she and "Ma-Ma Ginny" would take me to ride in her car *Blue Bonnet*—and no one else was allowed to go.

My Aunt Ellen was a classic; I was scared to death of her. I think it goes back to the time when I was about 3 and did not listen to her when she told me not to go near the road.

I was walking toward the highway in front of her house, she called for me to stop, and, of course, I did not. She trotted over, picked me up, and spanked me. That's not the end of the story, though. You see, I was not the only one who got into trouble that day, because when we got back to the house Ma-Ma Ginny fussed at her for spanking me. I loved my Ma-Ma Ginny! And, I loved Ellen.

Cheryl Whitlock Gaines (my sister): As I said earlier, I am the oldest of four. For the first five years of my life, I was the only child and grandchild in the house where I lived. Then, in 1966, **Cheryl Denise Whitlock** came along, and man did my life change. Sissy stole my thunder and has never given it back.

My siblings (L-R): Bryan Whitlock, Cheryl Whitlock Gaines, Me, and Phillip Whitlock

While I am the oldest, Cheryl is clearly the undisputed leader of the four Whitlock siblings. My two brothers and I are all scared of her.

* * *

Gibbs Memorial Baptist Church

I cannot write of Bostwick without talking about Gibbs Memorial Baptist Church. I do not know where to begin when discussing the little white church just beyond the left field fence of the town's baseball field. It means so much to me. That church and its members had so much to do with the things that are good in me.

Our church was not only our place of worship; it was at the center of most of the social activities I was involved in as a boy. When living in such a small town, you plan much of your social calendar around what is going on at church. Bible school, church camp, Royal Ambassadors (RAs), training union, hayrides, etc., were sources of great fun for us kids growing up. Those events, even though the adults had usually organized them for better and higher purposes, were times all of us could get together and have a good time.

Here are a few more of my personal recollections of our church:

- It was there that **Miss Lurene Alford** taught dozens of us "Do Lord," "This Little Light of Mine," and "Jesus Loves Me." This world needs more Miss Lurenes.
- **Miss Martha Jo Paxson** was always the Bible school director. *Attention, Salute, Pledge.*
- I remember **Mr. Hammond Calloway**, who was a leader in our church. When he prayed on Sundays, it sounded as if he was having a one-on-one conversation with God.
- I guess at one time or another, every person that taught a Sunday school class back then had to say the words, "Scotty, HUSH!"

- I have great respect for today's music directors, ministers of music and such; however, I feel that **Gene Ruark's** bellowing voice is the stick by which all choir directors must be measured.
- **Christmas Plays** – My favorite was when John Ruark and I starred, and brought the house down, in *"Christmas Comes to Detroit Louie."*
- Jack and **Carolyn Chandler** and **all the young adults** who took time with us kids. Heck, Jack even used to employ me on his farm, even though I probably wasn't much help. I owe Jack and Carolyn a great deal.
- Boy, I still miss **Robbie Paxson**. Robbie was several years older than my crowd. He was an athlete and a gifted pianist. He worked in the church with us young guys and played the piano for our youth choir. When I was only a college sophomore, we lost Robbie suddenly. He was a good man.
- **Youth choir practice** – There were about two dozen of us boys and girls that grew up together in Bostwick. Many of us sung in the Gibbs Memorial youth choir. Carolyn Chandler had the longest tenure as our "director." We were usually impossible for her to keep on task, but we had a ball at practices —*and hardly ever embarrassed her during a service.*
- **The back pews during preaching** – The two or three back pews on the preacher's right side of the church was where we young boys would usually sit for preaching. We talked, played, poked, and kicked throughout every service. And we did it while trying to have it appear that we were paying attention to the service. We were usually successful; but I do recall once when John Ruark's daddy (Marvin) got up from his seat and came to the back and sat

among us. Guess we might have overdone it that day.

Friendships

At the time I was growing up in Bostwick, there were many boys about my age, so I always had plenty of playmates. Some of those playmates grew into lifelong friends and brothers. Here are a few of them:

The Batchelor Boys: Right across the street from me lived **Travis, Mark,** and **Randy Batchelor.** I was six months older than Travis, who was a year older than Mark. Randy was born a year or so after Mark.

We played together regularly for our entire childhoods. Looking back, I realize that they were the best guys anyone could have had as neighbors. The three of them made many days of my childhood fun. And they were all fine athletes. In fact, Travis might have been the most gifted baseball player I ever played with. He could hit right- or left-handed, run, and throw. He was a natural.

Terrell Burge: I was the last of four boys born during the second half of 1961 in Bostwick. The four of us went to Sunday school and church together, were educated together, played sports together—you might just say we grew up together. First there was **Keith Nunn** (July), then **John Ruark** came along on the last day of August; three days later **Henry Terrell Burge** was born. I arrived in late November—even in being born, I always seemed to be coming in behind those boys. Throughout our growing up, Keith was always the fastest, John was probably the toughest, Terrell was the strongest, and then there was me.

Terrell (along with his older brother Allen) was one of my first regular playmates. We both lived in town, so we spent many days together. He was one of the most naturally-gifted athletes I ever saw. I am quite certain that if he had come along in the current era, Terrell would have been a big-time college athlete. He had the combination of strength and speed that would have made him a can't-miss prospect. Of the many things I remember about Terrell, it is what he did while we were in high school that I'll always remember most.

While in high school, Terrell found himself at a personal crossroad and made a profound choice. Late in his high school life, Terrell Burge, a rough and sometimes tough kid, found *real* religion and committed himself to being a minister. Since then, I have viewed him with such great respect and admiration. He, and his faith, are the real deal.

During his freshman year and my *second* freshman year of college, we roomed together at Truett McConnell College (now University). One night when we were looking for a parking place at the girl's dorm, I saw Terrell get out of the car I was driving, back up to a poorly parked Ford Pinto, squat down, lift it up, and scoot it over so we could park.

While we roomed together at college, I always respected Terrell's calling. I never allowed any of my friends to come to our room if Terrell was reading or studying, or if my friends were a bit too loud on a given night. Besides, if we had disturbed Terrell, he could have thrown us all out on our rears, and we could not have done one thing about it.

John Herschel Lill III: One of the cool things about growing up in a small town is that generation after generation grow up and remain friends. John's dad (Johnny) is a lifelong friend of my dad and John III is a lifelong friend of mine. In fact, my mom and dad were involved in introducing his dad to his mom.

When John and I were young, we'd play together while our parents played *Rook* in the dining room. When I was around 5, I was upset when John and his family moved away for a while, but after a few years they moved back. It was then that our friendship grew strong. Whether it was playing golf, water skiing, losing to him in ping pong or going to Athens on the weekend (because neither of us could get a date), I always had a good time when Lill and I were out and about.

Mr. John Lill, Me, and John Herschel Lill III

John Herschel Lill III is a good man and one of the smartest people I know. His parents, Johnny and Miss Mary, made a huge impact on my life. Their attitude of *family* is truly something special. They dragged me along all over the place. No matter if we were at Lake Hartwell (on the border of Georgia and South Carolina), at a Falcons game or in Myrtle Beach, Mr. and Mrs. Lill were always generous and welcoming hosts. When I was a boy, they made it easy for me to be John's friend.

* * *

John Marvin Ruark Jr.: It is no coincidence that in listing memories of some of my childhood friends I have saved John Ruark for last. Our close and uninterrupted friendship is now in its 55th year. As I have previously mentioned, generational family friendships are a perk of coming from a small town.

John's dad (Marvin) and my dad are lifelong friends, and the same goes for John and me.

Over our 55+ years of living, we've been through a little bit of everything together. We have cut up in Sunday school, sneaked up and played with Mrs. Hawk's (our first-grade teacher) carbon paper—I got caught, spanked, and cried (John got away), played little league baseball, went to car races, went to college, and laughed and cried together. Through it all, and we've both had our share of ups and downs, we have always managed to remain loyal to each other.

Me and John Marvin Ruark - You can't make old friends

When we were kids, I was *Barney* to John's *Andy*. We lived on opposite ends of town, about a mile apart. So until we became mobile (got bicycles or motorcycles), it was always an *occasion* when we got together. Once, in an effort to make it easier for us to get together, we started a tunnel that was to run from under his house all the way down to town where most of us lived. We had that tunnel going pretty well before we canceled the project. We had dug three or four feet when his ma-ma found out what we were doing and made us quit.

As we got older, we got to see more of each other. And when

school and work would allow, we had no problem finding all sorts of things to do and trouble in which to get.

There are countless stories that involve John Marvin Ruark Jr. and yours truly:

- There's the one of John and me and the motorcycle wreck. Afterwards, we decided to go to his Aunt Wynelle's house and clean up to avoid getting into trouble—that did not work out because our spill had nearly cut off my right ear (15 stitches).
- There's the one about our skipping three days of school in the 11th and 12th grade in order to go to the Daytona 500. We'd stay at the same hotel as my Uncle Pete— that's all I am at liberty to say about Daytona and the race trips. The rest remains classified.
- Of all the stories about the escapades of John Ruark and me, the one that has become part of Bostwick folklore is the *Tree Climbing Story* (see chapter 1). John has a version, and others have theirs.

Final Thoughts on Bostwick, Georgia

The great American songwriter Roger Miller penned the words, "Lord, when all my work is done, bless my life and grant me one *old friend*, just one *old friend*." Since first hearing that, I have always loved that thought. Today, those dear, wonderful folks in Bostwick provided me with more "old friends" than one man deserves.

* * *

Members of the Owl Nation

This book would be incomplete if I did not introduce you to the members of the Owl Nation. Following are just some of the people who were and remain so important to my life and career at Kennesaw State University.

The writings would go into volumes if I were mention everyone or go into detail about these special people, so I am going to provide somewhat of a CliffsNotes version.

Dr. Betty L. Siegel, President Emeritus of Kennesaw State University: Dr. Betty Siegel was KSU's second president. She held the office for 25 years. She is the greatest visionary that I know and is the *mother* of Kennesaw State Athletics. Prior to her arrival, our school did not have intercollegiate sports. Somehow, on day one, Dr. Siegel saw what was about to happen at Kennesaw College. She knew Kennesaw State University was inevitable. Her visionary leadership style took a commuter college of about 4,500 and morphed it into one of the United States' 50 largest universities. Very early in her tenure, as I said, she saw that Kennesaw needed intercollegiate athletics in order to offer a more complete college experience to the students. She hired Coach Spec Landrum to be the Owls' first athletic director. Coach Landrum took a shot on a 23-year-old softball coach, and the rest is...

Dr. Siegel also showed me that Kennesaw State was *home* back in the summer of 2000 when I flirted leaving Cobb County to try my luck at a *Power Five* school. She also introduced me to Dr. Bobbie Bailey (chapter 9). I love and respect "Miss Betty."

James "Spec" Landrum, Kennesaw College's first Director of Athletics: Father figure, mentor, and friend are how I describe my feeling towards this giant. He always gave me room in which to grow, encouragement, and praise. And, most of all, he gave me a chance. I miss him.

Dr. Mildred Landrum, KSU Professor (retired) and Coach

Landrum's Wife: Coach Landrum was scared to death of her (with good reason, the lady is most formidable). I too remain frightened of drawing her wrath. She gave me my first bit of professional advice, "Grow thicker skin Scott, or get out of coaching." I love you Dr. Landrum.

Dr. Dave Waples, Kennesaw State Director of Athletics (retired): He succeeded Coach Landrum and was my boss for 24 years. Upon Coach Landrum's foundation, Dave built a measuring stick (1988-2005) when it came to successful *small college* collegiate programs. He and Dr. Siegel also led our transition to NCAA Division I.

Despite his penurious spending habits and insistent *Monday morning quarterbacking*, he equipped each KSU program with what was requisite to be competitive. Of all the things that happened during his tenure (and there are many), the most recurring was that WE WON. Thanks Coach.

Ron Walker, Owls Head Women's Basketball Coach: From the autumn of 1986 until 1992, "Ronnie Chickie, Baby, Sweetheart" (*as I would call him when he'd get mad at me...he'd then laugh, and I'd be out of trouble*) successfully led our women's hoops team. He never had a losing season. I was his assistant coach for two years, but more importantly, he was my runnin' buddy (and I don't mean *jogging*) and friend. Ron was born to coach. He was very good at it.

Cancer took him from us in 1992, and I have yet to forgive it.

Roger E. Hopkins, KSU's Vice President for Finance: The man is Kennesaw State royalty. He was the person who fiscally shepherded Betty Siegel's vision. There was many a cabinet meeting disrupted when Mr. Hopkins would erupt with, "*Damn it Betty! Where are we going to get the money?*"

From the time when intercollegiate athletics was brought to

Kennesaw until his retirement, Mr. Hopkins worked closely with departmental leadership to strategically build a top-notch collegiate athletic program. All he did was help us win. He was a hell of a man.

Mike Carroll, Director of Academic Computing: A computer whiz, when slacking off, Mike and his friend Frank would make Kennesaw's first president, Dr. Horace Sturgis think that they were working hard by just turning on the reels of their computers (*this was the late 1970s*). When President Sturgis would see the reels spinning as he walked by their lab, he would always compliment them. That was Mike in a nutshell—half highly-intelligent professional and half con man.

When athletics arrived, he became a huge fan and a good friend. He left us too soon.

Chief Ted Cochran, Chief of Campus Police: For more than two decades, Chief was the head of campus's public safety department. He was also my first assistant coach. All we did was win. He is a great guy and an Owl for life.

Dr. Nancy King, Vice President for Student Success: A cutting-edge innovator in higher education, Dr. King helped invent the blueprint for courses aimed to enhance the first-year experience for college students. Her national accolades are seemingly endless.

She continues to be a role model and mentor. Man, she is so smart.

Phil Zenoni, Kennesaw's First Head Men's Basketball Coach: Phil is a good man. He even gave me a place to live once when I was down on my luck. While at KSU, his teams were well coached, did well academically, and never caused any problems. I will never fully understand why he was let go. When it happened, Phil understandably became disinterested with all things Kennesaw State, including me. We went years without any real contact, yet we lived in the same town. I am happy to report that Phil and I have reestablished our friendship. He is a member of the Kennesaw State Athletics Hall of Fame. I have great respect for him. I also once lost $63 to him playing putt-putt.

Greg Yarlett, Owls Second Head Men's Basketball Coach: I have a deep respect and fondness for Greg. He was a very loyal assistant to Phil Zenoni and handled his succeeding him with dignity. A fine coach in his own right, he became a victim of his loyalty, and his assistant coaches cost him his job.

Not having his contract renewed crushed Greg. He struggled for a while and we lost contact. I am so happy that he is again a part of my world. The *Big Dawg* is a good man!

Man, I still miss **Bill Hill**. (See chapter 7 for more on Bill.) As I shared in the chapter that I dedicated to our friendship, Bill Hill was KSU's Men's Golf Coach for a number of years. He was a buddy who possessed a wicked sense of humor. I think about him often. We lost both Bill and Ron Walker to cancer. Both were like family to me.

Mike Sansing, Head Baseball Coach: Mike Sansing is my friend, and the best coach (*of any sport*) that Kennesaw State has ever had. There are so many things that I could say about him, none bad.

For over a quarter century, we have been peers and *business* partners—our *business* was and is *WINNING,* and business has been kind to us. In the 1990s, our baseball and softball teams fed off one another—each winning two national championships and making numerous national tournament appearances. Though our approaches to coaching were extremely different, we both seemed to bring out the best in our athletes, the numbers speak for themselves (you can look 'em up). Mike's affable demeanor and my over-the-top personality meshed into a great tandem. Together our programs *moved the bar* for all sports at Kennesaw State, and for baseball and softball in any of the conferences in which we competed.

Our programs never engaged in petty jealousies, such as the, "His program gets more support than mine," crap that you can hear daily on just about any campus. Instead, we chose to embrace each other's successes and capitalize on them—the results were magic. For all you young professionals, there is a lessoned to be learned in there somewhere.

He is still out there each day coaching his heart out. And, Mike Sansing's heart is so big that he may coach forever.

Colby Tilley, KSU Women's Basketball Coach (retired): Life is so funny. In 1980, a friend of mine, Joe Gailey asked me if I would like to volunteer to keep statistics for the women's basketball team at Truett-McConnell Junior College. I agreed. It was then that I first discovered women's athletics and learned an appreciation for the female athlete. The head coach of that team was Colby Tilley.

Flash forward 15 years or so, and I was on the committee that hired Coach Tilley to become KSU's fifth women's basketball coach. After having record-setting careers at Truett and later Auburn-Montgomery, the guy who actually introduced me to coaching women's athletics was a peer. *And to this day, he still doesn't know whether to thank me or kill me for bringing him to KSU.*

Coach Tilley led our Owls from 1995-2012—17 seasons. His accolades from that tenure are too long to mention here. All he ever did was win. Over his 17 years, his teams won 290 games. Six other coaches—over 19 seasons—have won 277. In the six seasons since his retirement (2012-18), the program has earned just 58 victories. Need I say more.

He, *as many of us did*, bit the bullet and coached four seasons in his prime (2005-2009), during KSU's transition from Division II into Division I. During that time, due to NCAA transitions rules his teams were ineligible for the NCAA postseason, which understandably, limited recruiting. Three years later an administrator, *who was hell bent on recruiting KSU athletics in his own image*, told KSU's winningest women's basketball coach, that he was no longer the "right fit" to continue in his role and urged "retirement." What was Colby to do?

It has been six seasons and only 58 wins later—perhaps the administrator missed while assessing who fits where. With all due respect to the current KSU women's basketball coaching staff (they are fine, qualified people), Colby Tilley should have been allowed to coach here until he deemed himself to not be the "right fit." He was considerably more qualified to make that assessment than someone who had never coached, and besides, had earned that.

Bob Jenkins: He was the best damn director of athletic housing we ever had. Just ask Colby.

Alex Guilford, Men's Basketball Player (1988-90): Alex is a 5'9" (being generous) point guard from southwestern Georgia. During his time at Kennesaw, he played hard every day and was a fine student. Upon our meeting, I became a confidant and mentor. Today, we are good friends.

Neither of us worried about our beginnings. We chose to stay focused on where we were going. My career was a matter of record. Alex graduated and has served young people for nearly 30 years—as a teacher, high school administrator, and a volunteer basketball coach.

In spite of all of his professional success, his life's best work is his daily display of class and high character, and more importantly, his success as a husband and father. AG is a role model and a good man.

As I write, I am 56 and he just turned 50. Our friendship is in its 30th year.

David Moore, Student Athletic Trainer: He worked with me during the national championship years. He is a funny, loyal, intelligent fellow. Though he rarely meant to, his antics would regularly make the players and coaches laugh. Upon graduation, he went on to be a teacher and an athletic director. We remain in contact to this day.

Bill Gray, Assistant Softball Coach: Bill is the most underrated and underappreciated coach who has ever worked as an Owls softball coach. Here's why:

First: He joined my staff immediately after Don McKinlay's departure. For 13 seasons, Donny and I were lightening in a bottle, and Bill had to follow that act.

Second: By the time Bill arrived, I had gained a bit of notoriety and was getting opportunities to speak at camps and clinics all over the country—leaving Bill here to hold down the fort. Don never regularly faced that situation.

Third: During my run working with USA Softball (a great honor), Bill was left to do a yeoman's share of day-to-day stuff and most of the recruiting—then, suffer through my *backseat driving*.

In reflection, all of that was unfair. Bill did an incredible job at KSU and remains a dear friend. Bill Gray is a hell of a coach, a good family man, and I owe him so much. Love you Bill.

Tory Acheson, Kennesaw State's fourth Head Softball Coach: For many years, Tory Acheson was a formidable opponent—

first as the head coach at Wisconsin-Parkside, then in the same role at Tennessee Tech. Over the years, Tory has become like a brother to me—*he even read my NFCA Hall of Fame induction speech.*

In January of 2015, he became KSU's fourth softball coach. After working for 18 months cleaning up a mess left by my successor, he was rewarded by being fired in the summer of 2017. Though it can be accurately argued that some of the circumstances surrounding his departure were self-created, I feel that mean-spirited people, *with personal agendas,* are what ultimately brought him down. He deserved better, and there are some people who should be ashamed of themselves for trying to *climb the ladder* by stabbing a good man in the back.

Today, Tory is a very successful private hitting instructor. He remains *my brother.*

Professor Randy Stuart: Randy Stuart is a professor of marketing and professional sales. For several years, she served as the Faculty Athletic Representative for KSU's Athletic Department. We are good friends—even though we are quite the mismatched pair of socks. I am a Southern boy, born and bred. She is...well (since decorum prohibits me from sharing her self-description) let's just say that she is a non-protestant, female from Chicago.

Despite the differences of our origins, we enjoy discussing matters heavy and light. She occasionally will help me with the preparation of presentations/speeches. More importantly, she is a quarterly lunch companion. Most important, she is my buddy.

Jay Moseley, Men's Golf Coach: Jay Moseley was a coaching prodigy. He became the Owls Head Golf Coach while in his mid-20s, and I was paired up with the "The Kid" as his program administrator shortly after he arrived.

From autumn of 2010 until he left KSU to become *The* Ohio State University's head coach after the 2015 season, he taught me more about coaching millennials than anyone ever has. He's just that good.

More importantly, Jay and I formed a bond that was beyond athletics. He has become a friend. I love "The Kid" and his family. Ohio State is very lucky to have him.

Keith Schunzel, Women's Volleyball Coach: See everything that I said about Jay Moseley—then transpose it all to the sport of volleyball.

As I write (fall, 2018), Keith Schunzel is the best head coach on Kennesaw State's staff. He is right for his time and connects with young people. Though I know he is destined to one day receive the same type of call that Jay did, I am so glad he is an Owl and my friend.

Charlotte Doolin, my *Nanny*: Charlotte Doolin is the most organized and dependable person I know. Already a Kennesaw legend, I persuaded her to join the athletic department as the executive assistant to the director of athletics in 2010. She held that position until her retirement in 2018. She has never fully forgiven me for talking her into taking the role.

I truly felt that bringing Charlotte into our department would help establish a sense of daily structure and consistency that our organization was lacking at the time. I was right. She was incredible at what she did. She ran the place!

So why would she be mad at me? Well, there are numerous reasons for her contempt of my 2010 sales job, but there is one reason that sits atop her list. Upon her arrival, she learned that she had just became Scott Whitlock's *nanny*. Charlotte is simply the best at keeping scatter-brained administrators (*mentioning no names*) on task. And according to her, I was very much in need of her training.

Just as Mary Poppins helped the Banks' children learn life's lessons, Charlotte, upon her landing in athletics, began to teach me how to be an administrator. She is a very blunt and direct instructor.

It was one day during one of her lectures that I borrowed a line from Robert Downey's take of Sherlock Holmes, and replied to her rebuke by saying, "Yes, Nan-ny." She's been my "nanny" ever since.

Charlotte and I were a hell of a team. We got stuff done, while others were still talking about what they were going to do. What really worked for Charlotte and I is that her personality is perfect for me. She is the classic foil. As most know, I love to joust verbally with folks. Charlotte is as glib and quick-witted (almost) as people say I am. She can give as well as she gets, and I love that. Our banter gave us a certain rhythm that allowed us to communicate, work, and laugh—all at the same time.

Our office exchanges are legendary. She holds nothing back. To the uninformed, who might happen to overhear one of our discussions, it might seem that she is about to (justifiably) kill me for what I just did or said. They might even witness her throw a wad of rolled-up rubber bands at me. In reality, it was all a big joke to us. We did it to break the tension or just to make ourselves (and others) laugh.

"Bumbling idiot" is her default description of this author, and I roar each time it is spoken. I hope that our (now) eight-year argument never ends. My *nanny* is among my best friends and is a highly-trusted confidant. And, just like the Banks' kids, I cried the day my *nanny* left.

Charlotte's and my unique style of communication brought something to mind. Many in today's workplaces take themselves far too seriously. Others have become socially paralyzed by *political correctness* (PC) and other such crap. Many are so intimidated (by today's self-appointed *social police*—whoever the heck they are) that they are afraid to say hardly anything.

They feel they must display a cardboard of a personality while in public.

Oh, if I say, "yes ma'am" to a lady—I mean to a woman, I mean to a female, that might offend someone two offices down the hall, so I'll just say "yes" to my highly-respected coworker. Have we really grown to be that small-minded and emotionally fragile? Give me a break.

I am a rigid believer in being *situationally proper* in one's actions and words and I believe in the Golden Rule, but I am not going to fret over being PC for fear of offending people who are usually already just looking for something to be pissed off about. You cannot win with folks like that. Therefore, why bother? People who kowtow to these social bullies are nuts. Bullies do what bullies do, until someone says "enough" and stands up to them.

God put us here to be happy and comfortable while walking on this Earth. I feel that as long as my actions and words are appropriate and not threatening to others, what right do sourpusses—from today's social media gossip crazed, nitpicking, insecure, phony, self-righteous, narrow-minded portion of humanity—have to tell me how to talk? And, shame on anyone who lets them.

Matt Griffin, Senior Associate Athletic Director: "Pee-Wee" came to Kennesaw State when our university consolidated with Southern Polytechnic State University in 2015. At SPSU, Matt had been an athlete, graduate, head coach, and administrator. At the time of consolidation, he was the Hornets athletics director.

Matt and I are a great fit. We enjoy working together and have become dear friends. Our friendship is fire tested, and he is one of the few people that I truly trust. Matt is a genuine faith-led family man.

Matt is a compulsive worrier *and I love to push his buttons.* I am a coach who is late into the back nine of his career *and Matt still makes coming to work fun for me.* My faith, respect, confidence, and brotherly love for him has no bounds.

Scott Whitlock's Geriatric Posse: These are the people who have supported me throughout my career, but more importantly are now family.

Some of the proud members of my Geriatric Posse

Grace Register "Ma-Ma" – One of my life's most stabilizing influences and the grandmother to my children. For over one-half century, she and Pop were a match made in Heaven. I love her very much.

Moe and Pat Myers – Moe replaced Pop who replaced Pa-Pa (see chapter 11 for more). Pat is his loving and generous wife who graciously shares him with me for days at a time. Everybody should have a Moe.

Glen and Linda Sayne – Glen is my buddy. Linda is one of my reality checks. Linda, like my sister (Cheryl) and my nanny (Charlotte), is very unimpressed with me. I love that.

Linda and Glen Sayne

The Right Reverend Wayne D. Barton – Trust me, Wayne ain't no preacher, but he is the dearest of friends. We even got kicked out of the same family once. We have laughed and traveled together for more than 30 years.

Ernie and Carolee White – I met the Whites when Ernie joined KSU's faculty in the 1980s. He and my wife worked within the same department. As a former collegiate coach himself, Ernie gravitated toward us coaches. The two of us became friends. We are now family. Over the years, our families have played golf, went to concerts, vacationed, brought in the New Year, and everything else families do together. They have an open, standing invitation at our house, and we at theirs.

Tom and Lucy Sirmon – I miss Tom and to this day, *I love Lucy*.

Norm and Becky Frame – Our next-door neighbors of 25+ years, the Frames are just the best. Norm is a quiet gentleman and Becky has been godmother of every dog that we have ever owned.

Gene and Diane Neal – Gene and I enjoy a genuine relationship that was first formed by our mutual love for Linwood

Register Sr. (Pop)—*Gene and Pop worked together.* Gene and I play together. Diane is a lovely devout woman, who has no idea what to make of me, but she still lets Gene play with me for which I am grateful.

Diane and Deacon Gene Neal

Bill Hudson – Next to Don McKinlay and Bill Gray, Bill Hudson had more to do with my successful coaching career than anyone. Here is why: Kelly Rafter, Christina Caldwell, Janet Kearns, Lacey Gardner, and Brittany Matthews are just some of our pitchers that benefited from his expertise as an instructor. More than that, Bill Hudson has become a loyal and trusted friend. Though our relationship's foundation was formed on the softball field, it has become so much more than that. "Ole Bill" is a gentleman and an Owl.

Marty and Phyllis Rafter – The parents of the best pitcher I ever coached, the Rafters are a huge part of the KSU softball story. Phyllis was the de facto *team mom* for over a decade. I miss her dearly. Martin J. Rafter served as an official scorer, confidant, and volunteer assistant coach for the KSU softball team during much of my tenure. Marty is a good man and a good enough friend to be unafraid to tell me what I needed to hear. Friends like that are hard to find.

AND, MOST IMPORTANTLY
Every player that ever wore an Owls softball uniform: I

owe everything that I have enjoyed professionally to the incredibly special women who wore a KSU softball uniform from 1986 to 2013. I am forever grateful. Collectively, you created something special. I just happened to be lucky enough to have been at the right place at the right time, and you—**the players**—took me on an unlikely and remarkable journey.

Now that it's over and I look back, all the championships, plaques, and trophies mean far less than each time one of you called me "Coach." It was my highest professional honor to have been your coach.

Whereas I am confident that the Kennesaw State University softball program could have prospered and succeeded without Scott Whitlock, I am certain that *Coach* Whitlock would have never happened without each of you.

Thank you.

I love my Owls

ABOUT THE AUTHOR

Described as the "Will Rogers of softball," because of his unique way of sharing his insights, **Scott Whitlock** is recognized as one of the sport's finest coaches. His illustrious, 28-year career began in 1985, when Kennesaw State University hired him as assistant women's basketball coach and assistant slowpitch softball coach. In 1986, he took over as head softball coach and was instrumental in building one of the greatest college softball programs in the country. Whitlock was the driving force behind the program's successful transition from slowpitch at the NAIA level to fastpitch at the NAIA, NCAA Division II, and Division I levels.

Competing at the D-II level, Whitlock guided his teams to back-to-back national championships in 1995 and 1996. His 1999 and 2000 seasons marked one of the best two-year runs in softball history when his Owls combined for 108 wins against only 15 loses—a winning percentage of .878. For 12 consecutive years (1991-2002), Whitlock led KSU to a final top 10 national ranking. In his 21 seasons coaching fastpitch, Whitlock compiled an overall fastpitch record of 997-296 (.771), placing him near the top in most NCAA softball coaching categories. Additionally, he won 13 regional crowns and coached 51 All-Americans. Combined with his years as a slowpitch coach (153-15, .910), Whitlock finished with an overall record of 1,150-311 for a winning percentage of .787.

In 2005, Whitlock was inducted into the National Fastpitch Coaches Hall of Fame. He was also inducted into the Georgia Dugout Club Hall of Fame in 2010.

At the conclusion of the 2013 season, Whitlock retired as one of the all-time winningest and most respected coaches in NCAA softball. He remained on staff at KSU as its senior associate athletics director. In his current role, he works on the management of capital projects, as well as serving as the program administrator for men's golf, softball, women's golf, and volleyball.

His quick humor and affable personality are found at softball clinics throughout the country. His expertise in the field is sought out by his peers, aspiring coaches, and coaching professionals not only from the United States, but from around the globe.

Whitlock is an avid golfer, an aspiring fisherman, and a fan of college football and NASCAR. He is also a classic country music aficionado and admirer of Hank Williams Sr.

Whitlock's wife, Susan, is a member of KSU's faculty. The couple have two children, daughter, Lacey Bass (along with son-in-law Blayne) and son, Blake, one granddaughter, Blair, 4, and a baby grandson, Wyatt, who arrived in 2019.

ABOUT THE EDITOR

Jason Brown is a copywriter/copy-editor for HNTB, an infrastructure solutions firm. He previously served as the copy-writer for Kennesaw State University's College of Professional Education.
In 1996, Brown became KSU's first sports information student assistant—working under the sports information director within the athletic department. As part of this role, he supported Whitlock's softball program by writing bios and feature stories on coaches and players, keeping statistics, oper-ating the stadium scoreboard during home games, and occa-sionally traveling with the team. The two developed a strong bond over their love of sports and the hit TV show *Seinfeld*. Brown served in this capacity for three years until his gradua-tion from KSU, where he earned a bachelor's degree in media communications.

Prior to his roles at HNTB and KSU, Brown served in various capacities in sports media, marketing, and public rela-tions where he worked for organizations such as ESPN, Fox Sports, Atlanta Braves, Atlanta Hawks, and the former Atlanta Thrashers. Recently, he earned a Master of Arts in Professional Writing from KSU.

Originally from Miami, Florida, Brown now makes his

home in Roswell, Georgia, where he lives with his wife, Amethyst, their 3-year-old son, Maddux, and newborn boy, Kameron. He is also the author of *Margin Matters: How to Live on a Simple Budget & Crush Debt Forever* (www. YourMarginMatters.com).

Made in the USA
Middletown, DE
11 January 2020